The Disciplined Trader

The
Disciplined Trader

Developing Winning Attitudes

Mark Douglas

NEW YORK INSTITUTE OF FINANCE

Library of Congress Cataloging-in-Publication Data

Douglas, Mark.
    The disciplined trader : developing winning attitudes / by Mark
Douglas.
        p.   cm.
    ISBN 0-13-215757-8
    1. Stockbrokers—Attitudes.   2. Stock-exchange.   I. Title.
HG4621.D68   1990   90-30237
332.64—dc20   CIP

Printed in the United States of America

20   19   18   17   16   15

This publication is designed to provide accurate and authoritative information in regard to the subject matter covered. It is sold with the understanding that the publisher is not engaged in rendering legal, accounting, or other professional service. If legal advice or other expert assistance is required, the services of a competent professional person should be sought.
—*From the Declaration of Principles jointly adopted by a Committee of the American Bar Association and a Committee of Publishers and Associations*

ISBN 0-13-215757-8

ATTENTION: CORPORATIONS AND SCHOOLS

NYIF books are available at quantity discounts with bulk purchase for educational, business, or sales promotional use. For information, please write to: Prentice Hall Career & Personal Development Special Sales, 240 Frisch Court, Paramus, New Jersey 07652. Please supply: title of book, ISBN number, quantity, how the book will be used, date needed.

 NEW YORK INSTITUTE OF FINANCE
Paramus, NJ 07652

On the World Wide Web at http://www.phdirect.com

To Paula Webb for her love, understanding and being there throughout the process of writing this book.

Contents

Foreword ix
Preface xi
Acknowledgments xvii

Part I Introduction 1

1 Why I Wrote This Book 3
2 Why a New Thinking Methodology? 15

Part II The Nature of the Trading Environment from a Psychological Perspective 31

3 The Market Is Always Right 35
4 There Is Unlimited Potential for Profit and Loss 39
5 Prices Are in Perpetual Motion with No Defined Beginning or Ending 41
6 The Market Is an Unstructured Environment 49
7 In the Market Environment, Reasons Are Irrelevant 59
8 The Three Stages to Becoming a Successful Trader 65

Part III Building a Framework for Understanding Ourselves 79

9 Understanding the Nature of the Mental Environment 85

10 How Memories, Associations, and Beliefs
    Manage Environmental Information   99
11 Why We Need to Learn How to Adapt   121
12 The Dynamics of Goal Achievement   139
13 Managing Mental Energy   155
14 Techniques for Effecting Change   167

        **Part IV   How to Become a
        Disciplined Trader**   **181**

15 The Psychology of Price Movement   183
16 The Steps to Success   201
17 A Final Note   223

Index   225

Foreword

My unique position in the financial community has allowed me the rare opportunity to talk to and question thousands of traders, brokers, and trading advisors since 1979. I am not a broker or a letter writer. I am the chief executive officer of CompuTrac, a company that supplies technical analysis to stock and futures traders. I perceive my position as being neutral, one that allows people to open up and talk to me freely. I started trading for my own account in 1960 and very quickly became aware of the underlying psychological blocks to good trading and money management. This realization has been confirmed by all who have counseled with me.

As a result, I sincerely feel that success in trading is 80 percent psychological and 20 percent one's methodology, be it fundamental or technical. For example, you can have a mediocre knowledge of fundamental and technical information, and if you are in psychological control, you can make money. Conversely, you may have a great system, one that you have tested and has performed well for a long period of time, yet if the psychological control is not there, you will be the loser.

A good trader knows from experience that over a period of time he may engage in more losing trades than winning ones. But money management, and a careful assay of the risks protected by realistic stops, will keep the trader out of trouble and ensure that on the "big" moves, he will profit. Money management is composed of two essential elements: psychological management and risk management. Risk management stems from the psychological factors being truly understood by the trader and "in place" before risk is even considered.

I would especially caution new traders and market participants that reading and passively analyzing your motivations are certainly a necessity, but the acid test comes with active trading under pressure. Start slowly. Question every trade. What motivated it? How was the trade managed? Was it successful? Why? Did you lose? Why? Write down your assessment and refer to your comments before making your next trade.

At all major CompuTrac seminars I try to have a workshop leader address the attendees on the psychological aspects of trading. The grim reaper who kills off "your equity" and disappears with your profits is not the mysterious and ubiquitous "they" but a simple misguided "you." Medea said just before she murdered her children, "I know what evil I'm about to do, but my irrational self is stronger than my resolution." If this sentiment reflects your mind set when you trade, then *The Disciplined Trader* is definitely the type of book you should be reading.

What a pleasure to read this book. My own education cost me a lot "the hard way." I can read myself into the pages—that's me, that's me! Mark has carefully fashioned his book into a comprehensive logical dialogue. It reads as if you are at his side and he is explaining it as a friend, which I know you will enjoy. You are fortunate because you are taking the time now, before you have made a serious mistake, I hope, to learn about yourself and to study your craft. The traders who take the time to reflect and practice will survive and possibly prosper.

TIMOTHY SLATER
President
CompuTrac Software, Inc.

Preface

The Disciplined Trader is a comprehensive guide to understanding the psychology of self-discipline and personal transformation needed to become a successful stock or futures trader. This book will serve as a step-by-step guide to adapting successfully to the unusual psychological characteristics of the trading world.

I say "adapting" because most people venturing into the trading environment don't recognize it as being vastly different from the cultural environment in which they were brought up. Not recognizing these differences, they would have no way of knowing that many of the beliefs they acquired to enable them to function effectively in society will act as psychological barriers in the trading environment, making their success as traders extremely difficult to achieve. Reaching the level of success they desire as traders will require them to make at least some, if not many, changes in the ways they perceive market action.

Unlike other social environments, the trading arena has many characteristics requiring a very high degree of self-control and self-trust from the trader who intends to function successfully within it. However, many of us lack this self-control because as children we learned to function in a structured environment where our behavior was controlled by someone more powerful than ourselves, whose purpose was to manipulate our behavior to conform to society's expectations.

Thus, we were forced by external forces to behave in certain ways through a system of rewards and punishments. As a reward, we would be given the freedom to express ourselves in some desired manner. As a punishment, we would either be prevented from getting what we wanted, causing emotional pain, or we were inflicted with various forms of corporal punishment, causing physical pain. As a result, the only form of behavior control that we typically learned for ourselves was based on the threat of pain—either emotional or physical—from someone or something we perceived as having more power than ourselves. And since we were forced to relinquish our personal power to other people, we naturally developed many of our traditional resources for success (the particular ways in which we learned to get what we want) from the same mental framework. Accordingly, we learned that acquiring power to manipulate and force changes upon things outside of us was the only way to get what we wanted.

One thing you will learn as a trader is that the mental resources you use to get what you want in your everyday life will not work in the trading environment. The power and control that are necessary to manipulate the markets (make them do what you want them to do) are beyond all but a handful of individuals. And the external constraints that exist in society to control your behavior don't exist in the market environment. The markets have absolutely no power or control over you, no expectation of your behavior, and no regard for your welfare.

If, in fact, you can't control or manipulate the markets and the markets have absolutely no power or control over you, then the responsibility for what you perceive and for your resulting behavior resides only in you. The one thing you can control is yourself. As a trader, you have the power either to give yourself money or to give your money to other traders. And the ways in which you choose to do this will be determined by a number of psychological factors that have little or nothing to do with the markets. And this will be so until you acquire some new skills and also learn how to adapt yourself to suit conditions as they exist in the market environment.

To operate successfully in this environment you will need to learn how to control yourself in ways that may be completely alien to you.

You will also have to learn how to grant yourself the mental freedom to shift your perspective to notice alternative possibilities to getting what you want in the trading arena, regardless of your expectations of how you are going to get it. There are only a few traders who have come to the realization that they alone are completely responsible for the outcome of their actions. Even fewer are those who have accepted the psychological implications of that realization and know what to do about it.

Rarely do any of us grow up learning how to operate in an arena that allows for complete freedom of creative expression, with no external structure to restrict it in any way. In the trading environment, you will have to make up your own rules and then have the discipline to abide by them. The problem is, price movement is fluid, always in motion, quite unlike the highly structured events that most of us are accustomed to. In the market environment, the decisions that confront you are as endless as the price movements you intend to take advantage of. You don't just have to decide to participate, you also have to decide when to enter, how long to stay in, and under what conditions to get out. There is no beginning, middle, or end—only what you create in your own mind.

In addition to the negative psychological implications that accompany these decisions, you must be aware that even if you make the minimum financial commitment of one contract per trade (as in the futures market), there is an unlimited potential for profit as well as an unlimited potential for loss. From a psychological perspective, this means that each trade has the possibility of fulfilling your wildest dreams of financial independence, and simultaneously presents you with the risk of losing everything you own. The constantly changing price movement makes it extremely easy for you to ignore the risk and tempt yourself into believing you don't have to follow your own rules, this time.

Here is an environment that offers complete freedom of expression combined with unlimited possibilities and unlimited risk. If you place in it a participant who is oblivious to these psychological conditions (one who operates from a mental framework oriented toward external structure, constraints, and expectations), then what you have is a formula for emotional and financial disaster.

This grim scenario certainly explains why so few people ever make money as traders. Actually, almost all of those who make an attempt at trading completely underestimate the difficulty and consequently overestimate their ability to fulfill their inflated expectations. Therefore, most, if not all, people who trade inflict some degree of psychological damage upon themselves. I am defining "psychological damage" as any mental framework that has potential for generating fear.

Fear results from any belief about environmental conditions that has the potential to cause either physical or emotional pain such as stress, anxiety, confusion, disappointment, or betrayal. Painful emotional conditions are basically the result of unfulfilled expectations. Unfulfilled expectations create a conflict between a person's beliefs about the way things should be and the actual environmental conditions that don't match those beliefs. This conflict is expressed through our emotions in the form of pain that we generally label as stress, anxiety, confusion, and so on.

People seem to avoid pain instinctively by building up mental defenses against the intrusion of environmental information that would confirm the existence of any conflict. These defenses consist of denials, rationalizations, and justifications—all of which will result in perceptual distortion.

"Perceptual distortion" occurs when our mental system automatically distorts environmental information by shaping and selectively excluding certain information to compensate for the conflict between what we expect and what the environment is offering us. This will be done in such a way that we will believe a shared reality exists between ourselves and the outside environment, thus avoiding any pain. I am defining a "shared reality" as a correspondence between one's beliefs about the environment and the actual environmental conditions that exist.

If you are distorting market information, you are not sharing a reality with the markets, and you are also indulging yourself in an illusion, to the extent that you hide from the possibility of disappointment. At this point, you would be setting yourself up for what could be called a "forced awareness." Obviously, if the markets are doing something other than what you are allowing yourself to perceive (because some, if not most, of the information the markets have to offer won't validate what you want or hope), then something has to give. These distortions will continue until there is such a disparity between your acquired mindset and the conflicting market information that the mental defenses (illusions) will break down. This usually creates a state of shock, where you may wonder how things could get so bad so quickly.

In such a situation, the market forces you to confront your illusions of a shared reality, creating a painful forced awareness. At some point in your trading career you will need to understand how all of us, because of our common upbringing, try to control market events through our perception of what we think will happen next and then rigidly hold on to these expectations. This is where you need to learn how to gain the kind of mental flexibility that allows you to shift your perspective to be aware of other alternatives and possibilities. You may not be able to control the markets, but you can control your perception of them in order to achieve a higher degree of objectivity, resulting in a higher degree of shared reality with the markets.

As painful as these forced awarenesses may be, they are not likely to deter you from being attracted to the opportunities the markets have to offer. However, the cumulative psychological effect on you will be very negative. If you have suffered through several forced awarenesses, your perception of market activity will eventually become heavily weighted towards avoiding pain instead of seeking opportunity. Your fear of losing money, being wrong, or missing an opportunity will become your primary motivation to act or not act.

Now, there are several major problems that result when fear becomes a motivation to do or not do something. First, it will limit your range of perceived opportunities by narrowing your focus of attention, keeping it on the object of your fear. This means that out of all available market information, you will only perceive information that will, in effect, validate what you fear the most. Your fear will systematically exclude from your awareness market information that would indicate the existence of other alternatives and opportunities.

As you begin to understand the negative relationship between fear and perception, you might be surprised to learn that in your attempts to avoid losses, you actually create them. Fear will also limit your range of responses to any given situation. Many traders suffer considerably when they know exactly what they want to do but, when the moment to execute arrives, find themselves completely immobilized.

Before anyone can become successful in an environment with the unstructured character of the trading environment, one needs to develop a supreme sense of self-confidence and self-trust. I am defining self-confidence as an absence of fear and self-trust: knowing what to do at the moment it needs to be done, and then doing it without hesitation. Any hesitation will only create self-doubt and fear. To whatever degree self-doubt exists as a state of mind, to that same degree you will feel fear, anxiety, and confusion.

The negative experiences that result from trading in a state of fear, anxiety, and confusion, will create or add to an already-existing belief of inadequacy and powerlessness. Regardless of how hard any of us may try to hide from others what is going on, we obviously can't hide our results from ourselves. If the market's behavior seems mysterious to you, it's because your own behavior is mysterious and unmanageable. You can't really determine what the market is likely to do next when you don't even know what you will do next, regardless of what you may perceive or want.

The few successful traders who have, in some way, transcended these psychological obstacles have been generous with their one-line gems of trading wisdom: "Learn to take a loss," "Go with the flow," "The trend is your friend," "Cut your losses and let your profits run," "To know the markets you need to know yourself," and on and on. *The Disciplined Trader* fully explores, breaks down, and then organizes the psychological components of this advice into a step-by-step learning process, a process that takes you through the various stages necessary to orient yourself successfully to the trading environment. This book will explain to you what skills are necessary, why you need to understand them, and most important, how to go about learning them.

This book is organized in four sections. The first consists of the first two chapters and serves as an introduction. The second consists of Chapters 3 through 8 and defines the problems or challenges of becoming a successful trader. The third section consists of six chapters that will give you the basic insight you will need to identify what has to be changed in your mental environment and what you can do to change it. The fourth section consists of Chapters 15 and 16 which put everything together into a unified framework to develop specific trading skills. You will learn how to observe market action from an objective perspective, determine where you need to limit yourself, and establish the steps you will need to take to expand those limitations in a productive and psychologically healthy way.

Acknowledgments

Most people are probably well aware that writing a book is a very difficult task, one that often requires the help and support of a number of people in the author's life. There are a number of people I want to acknowledge as being instrumental in helping me make this book a reality including my parents, John and Helen Yosin; my brothers and sister—Craig, Dean, and Sandy Yosin—for all their love and support; Brad Johnson, my partner in Trading Behavior Dynamics, for all of his patience and kindness; Jim Sutton, Bonnie Marlowe, Jake Bernstein, Elizabeth McKinsey, Michael Headley, Steve Sukenik, and Jack Carl for helping me get started; all of the traders that I have worked with over the last six years, especially Jim Griswold, Jerry Stahlnecker, Jack Brassuel, Steve Bianucci, Mike Gamble, and Chuck Pettet for their friendship and support; Tim Slater for giving me the opportunity to express myself as a speaker and a writer; Rich Miller for his support and being a good friend; Lori and Nikki Marlowe for the happiness they brought into my life; and most of all, my friend and fellow author Kurt Leland for everything he has taught me and for showing me the way.

PART I

Introduction

CHAPTER 1

Why I Wrote This Book

Since I started working on this book—in the summer of 1982—nearly every dimension of futures trading has exploded in growth. There are brand new exchanges, new contracts, more advisory and news services, an increasing variety of books and publications, and ever more sophisticated technical trading systems, most all of them with computer applications to make it easy to track the markets. However, even with this tremendous growth in services related to trading, one inescapable fact remains: there is still a very small group of sophisticated traders who take the greatest percentage of profits out of the markets, making well over 90 percent of all the other traders net losers year-in and year-out.

In futures trading for every dollar of profit gained by one trader, there has to be an equivalent dollar lost by another trader. If a few traders are consistently making money on a grand scale, then their profits have to be coming directly out of the pockets of the thousands of other traders who very faithfully contribute to their daily winnings. Some of these very successful traders are public figures, but most are only known in the Chicago or New York areas. Needless to say, everyone wants to know what they do and how they do it.

There must be a difference between these two groups of traders—the small minority of winners and the vast majority of losers who want to know what the winners know. The difference is that the traders who can make money consistently on a weekly, monthly, and yearly basis approach trading from the perspective of a mental discipline. When asked for their secrets of success, they categorically state that they didn't achieve any measure of consistency in accumulating wealth from trading until they learned self-discipline, emotional control, and the ability to change their minds to flow with the markets.

First, I want to point out that self-discipline, emotional control, and learning to change one's mind after making a commitment are all psychological issues that have nothing to do with news services, advisory services, new exchanges, or technical or fundamental trading systems—computerized or not.

Second, from my trading experiences, observations, and research, I have discovered that all traders—both winners and losers—seem to share some very common experiences. Either in the beginning or at some point early in their trading career, all traders experience confusion, frustration, anxiety, and the pain of failure. The few traders who pass through this phase to accumulate wealth are those who eventually confront and work through some very difficult psychological issues about what it means to be a trader, and this process of realization and change normally takes several years, even for the best of them.

If self-discipline and emotional control are the keys to success, they are also not necessarily traits any of us are born with. On the contrary, they are characteristics we acquire by learning certain mental skills. Acquiring these mental skills is often the result of a trial-and-error learning process that can be very costly financially and usually filled with emotional pain and suffering. The biggest problem with a trial and error approach in trading is that most people lose all their money before they get through the process. And other traders who have enough money to keep on trading never fully recover from the effects of the psychological trauma they have inflicted on themselves to ever learn how to trade successfully on a consistent basis. This leaves only a relatively small number of people who make it.

All the great traders, both past and present, have found it very difficult to explain what it is they do, how they do it, and more important, the progression of steps they took to get where they got. Many would gladly share with others what they know about the market and its behavior but not necessarily about their behavior as individuals. They would, however, often caution those who sought their wisdom to understand that all the market knowledge in the world won't do them any good until they learned what can be called self-discipline and emotional control, without necessarily being able to explain what they were.

For instance, "Cut your losses short" is great advice that is often given as an axiom of trading wisdom. But how do you explain to someone the steps needed to learn how to do that? Especially when he is interacting with an environment that is in perpetual motion and will always offer him the possibility that the market can come back and make him whole, if he is in a losing trade. If you take into consideration that his money and self-esteem are at stake and the market coming back is always a viable possibility, regardless of how remote it may be, then you can see how difficult it is to explain why he needs to "cut his losses." It is even more difficult to explain how he can do it in a way that suits his unique psychological makeup.

The easiest way to explain how to apply this type of wisdom, without actually explaining it at all, is to say, "Well, if you want to be a successful trader, you need to learn self-discipline and emotional control." I don't believe this type of vague advice was intentional, however, for principally two reasons. First, self-discipline and emotional control are abstract concepts that are not easily explained or understood. We all hear or read the words a lot, but ask anyone you know to define either of these concepts, and you'll probably get a blank stare.

Second, today's successful traders started out their journey without maps, signposts, or guidelines or the benefit of knowing exactly where they had to end up, from a psychological perspective, to accumulate their fortune. They had to explore the trading world through a means of self-reflection and readjustment that was very demanding and time consuming. One could say they more or less stumbled through it learning from each mistake, many small and others that were devastating both financially and emotionally.

At some point, they probably realized that something about themselves had changed because the normal kind of market activity that once had a very negative emotional impact on them, like anger, stress, anxiety, and fear, just didn't have that same effect any longer. They must have gained some measure of confidence in themselves to respond appropriately to all possible market conditions because there is a direct correlation between a person's level of confidence and the negative emotions mentioned. Confidence and fear are states of mind that are similar in nature, only separated by degree. As a person's level of confidence increases, his or her degree of confusion, anxiety, and fear dissipates proportionately.

This confidence would naturally develop as people learned to trust themselves to do whatever needed to be done, without hesitation. As a result of this kind of self-trust, they would no longer need to fear the seemingly unpredictable and erratic behavior of the markets. However, the main point I am making here is that the process of change that took place was in the mental environment and psychological makeup of each individual trader; the markets didn't change, the tools that were used didn't change, the trader did.

Now, when traders go through a transition in their personal development and learn a new skill on a trial-and-error basis, it is unlikely that they would keep a detailed record of the steps to that learning process, especially if that process was characterized by pain, anxiety, and frustration. Obviously, if someone doesn't know exactly how they acquired the skills they now have, then, naturally, it would be extremely difficult for them to explain to someone else how they got them.

Besides, when it comes to trading, once someone is making the kind of money he had always dreamed of, there isn't much incentive to spend the time and energy necessary to break down these abstract skills into an effective learning process from which others can derive some benefit. Developing educational programs to explain how to become a successful trader requires a completely different set of skills from the skills necessary to be a trader. As will be explained in a moment, the learning process and the kind of personal transformation that was necessary to enable me to write this book was distinctly different from the kind of learning process I experienced as a trader to realize why a book like this needed to be written. One learning process was chosen and the other was forced.

What I mean by forced is, I had to lose my house, my car, and practically everything else I owned to learn some of the ways in which I needed to change my perspective to operate in the trading environment effectively. Losing all my possessions was a complete life-altering experience, an experience that taught me a lot about the nature of fear and the debilitating effects it has on a person's ability to trade effectively.

The kind of insight I gained as a result of this experience is the type of learning process I call a forced awareness. This is where the nature and characteristics of the environment I was operating in were much different from what I believed they were, first out of ignorance, and because I put up mental defenses to block my perception of certain information. Eventually I was forced by the markets to acknowledge many things about myself that I otherwise wouldn't consider. When all the external symbols that represented a major part of my identity were gone, I didn't have any other choice and was forced to perceive myself in new and different ways.

These events occurred in March 1982. At the time, I was an account executive with Merrill Lynch Commodities at its Chicago Board of Trade office. Less than a year before, in June 1981, I moved from the suburbs of Detroit where I was enjoying, at least financially, a very successful career in commercial property and casualty insurance. I left Michigan and success to move to Chicago and be a trader. I went to work for Merrill Lynch because I didn't have enough money to buy a seat at the Board of Trade or the Chicago Mercantile Exchange and didn't know that you could lease seats at that time.

I had an expensive apartment on the gold coast of Chicago and a Porsche; I was maintaining a house in an affluent suburb of Detroit that my girlfriend and her two daughters were living in; and I was driving or flying back and forth between the two cities almost every weekend to visit them. I was under extreme financial pressure to succeed because my life-style expenditures were far and away in excess of what I could afford. Unless I made it big as a trader, it would be very hard to reconcile some of the decisions I made to put myself in that kind of a situation.

By the time I moved to Chicago I had already been trading for over two years. Twice, before moving, I lost all my trading capital. Of course, I would quickly save up and start again. My brief periods of success and few winning trades were enough to justify that I continue trying. Once I was very close to making over a quarter of a million dollars on a trade, but I pulled out of it just before the big move. This devastated me, but I also became completely hooked on trading and even more determined to be successful. From that experience I decided to buy all the books I could get and attend all the seminars I could afford.

Something stated in virtually all the books I read was that it is very difficult to learn how to trade or sustain any success if one is under a great deal of financial pressure—meaning don't expect to become a successful trader if you have limited trading capital or if you are trading with money you can't afford to lose. I was obviously violating both these rules because I had very little trading capital relative to my life-style that I absolutely could not afford to lose. Also I had a lot of other evidence that the odds were not exactly in my favor.

I came to Chicago because I believed that if I could get close to the action and meet people who knew how to trade, I could then learn from them. I was in for a very rude awakening. I was at Merrill Lynch Commodities, its second largest commodity office, with 38 account executives. At first I was shocked to find out only one of the account executives had any experience trading his own money. Then I was further shocked to learn that none of these account executives had any customers who were making any money. In fact, the typical customer lost his original stake within an average of four months.

My next major disappointment came when I began to meet and make friends with as many floor traders as possible, believing that if the guys up in the offices don't know how to make money, the floor traders certainly must. Again, I found the same conditions that existed up in the offices. Other than a handful of floor traders who had a reputation and a mystique that everyone seemed to be in awe of, I couldn't find one person who was making money consistently, who wasn't confused or knew what he wanted to do and then did it, without first having to ask everyone around him for confirmation that he was doing the right thing. I am not implying that I didn't meet traders who at some point in the day hadn't made money. They just couldn't keep it. I knew many traders who could make $2,000 or $3,000 the first couple of hours of trading. But they would always lose it back, plus more, a short time afterward.

Everybody seemed to be suffering from the same kinds of problems and mistakes that nobody really recognized as problems. Obviously, the nature of the markets made it easy not to have to confront anything that otherwise might be perceived as a problem because the next trade always had the possibility of making everything else in one's life seem irrelevant. Why deal with anything if the next trade can make you rich? All the traders I knew, including myself, were affected by this type of "big-trade" mentality. In fact, my big-trade mentality was so pervasive that I would refuse to take profits of $500 or $750 in many trades even when I knew that's all there was to be made. This may sound absurd, but I wouldn't take profits of such small amounts, because, at that time, it felt as if the market was insulting me by offering such paltry sums compared to what I needed or expected.

As my financial problems grew, so did my desperation. And I certainly wasn't comforted by anything I saw going on around me. But I still held on to the belief that I could trade out of these difficulties. That is until March 1982; by then it was all over. A mere eight months after moving to Chicago to pursue my dreams of financial independence, I had nothing left except my job, apartment, clothes, a television, and a bed.

Practically overnight, almost all the symbols that validated my identity were gone. What I mean is, a big part of my self-concept was made up of my possessions like my house, my car, and especially my credit. Maintaining flawless credit was something I had always been proud of. Now I found myself without any of these things. As I've already pointed out, it's not as if there hadn't been plenty of evidence to suggest the possibility of this happening, because there had been. But there was a part of me that wouldn't allow a direct confrontation with this evidence or the implications. It was just too easy to make excuses for all the things going on around me that didn't add up.

Refusing to confront or consider the implications of all the conflicting information created a great deal of stress. And to compound the situation, I had this intense fear that I would lose everything. But again, I did everything possible to hide this fear and put it somewhere in my mind where I couldn't feel it. Yet, there must have been a part of me that sensed my impending fall. Why else would I have been so consumed with fear? But how could I face any of this when I had no way of reconciling the imbalance that losing all of these things would create? What I mean is the imbalance between what I believed about myself and the things that validated these beliefs. Who would I be after all these things were gone?

Well it didn't take me very long to find out. As my financial condition deteriorated to critical levels, my mental defenses also began to break down. I eventually accepted the inevitability of doing what I believed was the ultimate act of failure and filed for bankruptcy.

There were a lot of things that changed inside of me as a result of this experience. And like any one else forced to deal with major changes in his or her life, I learned a lot about myself. The first thing that happened, which was quite surprising, was that the stress dissipated. Actually I was overcome with a great sense of relief with nothing to anticipate, dread, or try so desperately to defend against. I was living through my worst fear and found there really wasn't anything about the situation that I couldn't deal with. It wasn't nearly as bad in reality as I imagined it would be. I was still alive and healthy, I was able to think and function, and I started to appreciate my ability to think as my greatest asset.

This sense of appreciation began to grow into a deeper level of understanding about the basic nature of my identity. For the most part, I grew up believing that who I was consisted of the things that I owned. The more possessions I owned, the more of a person it made me. What I began to realize is that I was more than the things I had accumulated. When the facade was stripped away, it allowed me to sense this deeper dimension that, up to this point, I had only the slightest inkling of. These new awarenesses, in turn, helped me understand how being wrong and losing something didn't in any way diminish me as a person. I was beginning to learn that there was a certain freedom in granting myself permission to be wrong and maybe there was no such thing as a failure, unless something positive and useful isn't learned from the experience.

However, I didn't relate these personal experiences because I thought they were particularly unusual, except for one. Everyone knows there are many traders who lose everything they own, and even though some of them will come to the same kind of awarenesses about themselves, they wouldn't necessarily be able to do it as a trader, considering the financial requirements. I, too, was not in a financial position to keep on trading, except that I still had my job at Merrill Lynch. In fact, for me it was business as usual, as if nothing at all had happened. I certainly wasn't about to announce to my customers or anyone in the office that I had just filed for bankruptcy. My job as an account executive was one of the few things I had left, and as far as I was concerned, it depended on me being a good trader.

This is the one key difference for me that ultimately lead to the creation of this book. I was fortunate enough to be able to keep on trading (although not with my own money) while these major psychological changes were taking place, putting me in a unique position to examine and study the various ways in which the condition of my inner psychological environment affected what I experienced in the outer physical environment.

This relationship between inner and outer isn't always that apparent but in this situation it was inescapable. I learned that the markets offer the trader an opportunity to profit from price movement, and these opportunities are basically in perpetual motion. It is an environment where the individual has the freedom to create his own results, unimpeded by many of the constraints that exist in everyday social life. These never ending opportunities make the market a perfect mirror of the trader's attitude. What the trader sees in that movement and what he can do about it the markets have no control over. All the choices and all the power to turn these choices into experience reside in the mind of each trader.

For example, if I perceived the market as a threat, afraid of what it might take away from me, it wasn't because the outside conditions were actually threatening me in some way. It became very apparent to me that my fear was a result of my inability to anticipate events or act in a way that most appropriately served my best interests. It was only the lack of trust I had in myself to do what needed to be done that I was really afraid of.

Furthermore, I discovered that my mental framework was structured to avoid losses at all costs and in my desperate attempts to do so, I actually created them. You can think of it this way: none of us has the mental capacity to be aware of everything going on in the environment at once. The environmental information we focus our attention on, out of all that exists, will be the information that has the most importance to us. As we allocate more and more of our attention to certain kinds of information, because of its importance, we are at the same time systematically excluding other types of information from our awareness. I created my losses instead of avoiding them simply because I was trying to avoid them.

Instead of being positively focused on market information that would indicate the potential for opportunity, I was more concerned with information that validated what I feared the most. As a result, a great deal of market information pertaining to other possibilities and opportunities that existed in any given moment completely escaped my attention, passing me by. The only way I could have perceived these opportunities (other than after the fact) would have been to let go of whatever was causing me to divert my attention away from what was happening in the market "now."

I had no way of knowing what I was missing out on until my beliefs about the significance of losses and being wrong started changing. Once this shift in perspective occurred, I started to notice behavior characteristics of the market and relationships between those characteristics that I was otherwise totally oblivious to.

At some point, I realized that because I had already lost everything, I really didn't have anything to fear, and, as a result, I inadvertently learned one of the most important lessons to becoming a successful trader: how to "accept" a loss without any negative consequences. No guilt, anger, shame, or self-punishment.

As my fear of losing dissipated, I was seeing and experiencing a different market because I was different. It was as if someone had removed blinders, which I didn't know existed, from my eyes. Up till then, my trading had always been affected by my fears. I didn't have the slightest notion of what it would be like to trade without fear or that doing it was even a possibility and least of all, that it was, in fact, necessary to be successful.

What also became very apparent to me was the extent to which all of my fears had effectively blocked me from understanding why it was so absolutely necessary to have some clearly defined trading and money management rules that must be followed. It was all starting to make sense. The more I followed my rules the more I trusted myself. The more I trusted myself the more I could focus my attention on subtle relationships in the market's behavior to learn new things about the market helping me become a better trader. Eventually I could gauge the positive effects these new attitudes had on my ability to shift my perspective and flow with the markets. The less I cared about whether or not I was wrong, the clearer things became, making it much easier to move in and out of positions, cutting my losses short to make myself mentally available to take the next opportunity.

By June 1982 I was starting to make consistent money for my customers who relied on me for their trades. Not a lot of money by most trader's standards, but steady. I was having winning days that were turning into winning weeks and months. Then sometime in August 1982 I thought of writing a book or at the very least developing a seminar to explain to other traders what I had discovered for myself.

In the area of education there was a definite void in the market. There really wasn't any material that addressed trading psychology at a deep enough level of insight to effectively help someone understand why success was so elusive. I wrote this book to address what I believe is a critical need for people who want to trade the futures of stock markets to have an organized, systematic, step-by-step approach to learn the mental skills necessary to accumulate wealth as a trader. The secret to this approach is learning a new thinking methodology.

CHAPTER 2

Why a New Thinking Methodology?

It is my intention in this chapter to demonstrate clearly how a typical social upbringing that instills in the individual certain values and beliefs that make up a thought methodology used for being successful is not practical or functional and is inconsistent with the methods necessary to be successful in the trading environment. Someone attempting to operate in the trading environment in all the familiar ways that would assure getting what they want will likely find themselves in a constant state of frustration, anxiety, and fear, wondering what is wrong or thinking something must be wrong with them.

The irony is, of course, that, on the surface, trading looks so simple, when in fact most people will find it to be the most difficult endeavor they ever undertake. Success will always seem so close, and yet always so elusive. And this frustration will continue until the trader adapts to the conditions that exist in the trading environment by learning a new thinking methodology, one that works most effectively in that environment and not what he thinks will work based on his cultural and social upbringing.

Perhaps many of you reading this book have heard about a seminar being offered where you can learn how to walk barefoot over a 20-foot bed of red-hot coals. The people who developed the method to make it possible did so on the assumption that the achievements of people who do things very well and excel beyond what other members of the same culture of society would consider possible do so as the result of a specific way they think—a methodology in which their beliefs are in some way different from everyone else's. This methodology can be broken down into a system that can be learned and subsequently taught to others. The only difference between those who excel and those of mediocre achievement is that one group has learned a thinking methodology that has not occurred to the other.

With this hypothesis, it is my understanding that the people who developed the program went to the South Pacific and sought out those who demonstrated an ability to walk over hot coals with their bare feet—without any physical damage whatsoever. Upon finding a few of these South Pacific "fire-walkers," the program developers proceeded to analyze their beliefs and attitudes so as to arrive at a thinking methodology they could teach in the United States.

I'm sure I don't have to point out the physical and emotional implications of attempting to walk over a red-hot bed of coals with your bare feet. The fear generated over just the thought of doing it would normally be overwhelming. The potential physical damage to your feet—with the possibility of being crippled for the rest of your life—is quite real. And yet, as presented by several news organizations, both television and print, people from all walks of life involved in the seminar accomplished what we would universally agree to be a tremendous feat. They overcame their fear and walked 20 feet over a bed of hot coals.

Now, I'm not going to have you fire-walking the futures pit, but habits of thought die hard. And to make way for the new thinking methodology I offer as a means of excelling as a trader, you will have to question some of your beliefs and probe deeply rooted concepts of what is possible. Sometimes only a thorough mental "house cleaning" can help you throw away failure to make room for success. And exposing yourself to information that may cause you to ask yourself "what if it were true" is the first step to any mental cleansing process.

For many reasons, which will be explored in greater depth in Part II, it rarely, if ever, occurs to the beginning trader that the markets confront him with an environment that is categorically different from anything he is accustomed to or trained to deal with effectively by society. For example, the markets can be looked at as a never-ending event, always changing, virtually without structure, in perpetual motion, with an unlimited potential for profit as well as loss in every trade.

The psychological impact on the individual interacting with such an environment is formidable—especially when you consider the many ways in which all of us typically go about structuring our lives with highly defined boundaries, limits, and rules, so things stay basically the same. For most people, a static environment is a fundamental component of their sense of security and well-being.

Not only can the markets destroy a person's sense of security by forcing the trader to confront, on a moment-to-moment basis, his lack of acceptance of change, but they also produce an emotional environment of considerable competitiveness and stress. There's the compulsive need to win millions, with the simultaneous fear of financial devastation. The markets tease a trader with the very real possibility of fulfilling his grandest dreams of financial independence and at the same time stand ready and willing to take away everything he owns—and more.

Furthermore, the principles of time, effort, and reward associated with most job situations simply do not apply with the markets. For example, many jobs offer an unchanging reward, regardless of effort, because of hourly wages or yearly salaries. For a trader, effort can be irrelevant, and there is virtually no relationship between time and reward. A trader can be stunned with a windfall profit in a matter of seconds for making one simple decision and the only energy expended was mental.

Initially, you may think what could be wrong with making a lot of money in minutes or seconds. A lot! Whether you're aware of it or not, most if not all of us grow up with highly structured belief systems about the conditions under which we deserve to receive money. In fact, many people because of their childhood conditioning and religious training believe they don't deserve any money they didn't work for.

Certainly, making a lot of money in a very short period of time with no effort expended does not fall within the definition most people have about working for their money. So how does someone reconcile windfall profits against these structured work beliefs, especially when they're probably not even aware of them or would not take them into consideration if they were? This kind of mental conflict usually gets reconciled by the trader finding some clever, ingenious, or mundane way of giving his money back to the markets.

Not adjusting to the differences between the cultural and trading environments or just being unaware that differences exist can certainly account for many of the trading errors committed by the majority of traders. Yet, a thinking methodology can not only redefine the market's behavior in understandable terms to avert such mistakes, it can also manage most, if not all, typical undisciplined, emotional reactions to that behavior.

CULTURALLY LEARNED BEHAVIOR THAT RESULTS IN AN UNSUCCESSFUL TRADING EXPERIENCE

In an emotionally charged situation that requires split-second decision making (which could lead to failure of some kind), there's little time to compare the present event with previous market experiences. You probably wouldn't even notice if you had behaved similarly in the past and suffered the same disastrous consequences. Because the present situation is so immediate, you may have no concept of how typical and even thoughtless your behavior may be.

In fact, it may be news to you that there are only a limited number of such typical reactions leading to failure. Being able to recognize them can prevent you from repeating past mistakes without losing any of that time so necessary for split-second decisions.

The following typical trading errors have a specific cause rooted in a thinking methodology that can be changed.

1. Refusing to define a loss.

2. Not liquidating a losing trade, even after you have acknowledged the trade's potential is greatly diminished.

3. Getting locked into a specific opinion or belief about market direction. From a psychological perspective this is equivalent to trying to control the market with your expectation of what it will do: "I'm right, the market is wrong."

4. Focusing on price and the monetary value of a trade, instead of the potential for the market to move based on its behavior and structure.

5. Revenge-trading as if you were trying get back at the market for what it took away from you.

6. Not reversing your position even when you clearly sense a change in market direction.

7. Not following the rules of the trading system.

8. Planning for a move or feeling one building, but then finding yourself immobilized to hit the bid or offer, and therefore denying yourself the opportunity to profit.

9. Not acting on your instincts or intuition.

10. Establishing a consistent pattern of trading success over a period of time, and then giving your winnings back to the market in one or two trades and starting the cycle over again.

SKILLS TO BE ACQUIRED

To excel in any activity—whether it is mental, such as trading, or physical, such as swimming—we need to learn specialized skills. These skills give us the necessary requirements to look at, think about, and behave toward events in a manner different from what we may be used to or what we may have been taught.

However, beyond the sheer mechanics of the activity—which just about anyone can master—lies a particular thinking methodology or strategy that leads to excellence. Although few people have it, such a thinking methodology can nevertheless be learned.

Any thinking methodology requires a series of approaches to goals and problems. These approaches might be better described as mental techniques, even skills of thought application. For example, one such skill might be the ability to identify those conditions that are conducive to making a common trading error before it actually happens. Other techniques or skills include:

1. Learning the dynamics of goal achievement so you can stay positively focused on what you want—not what you fear.

2. Learning how to recognize the skills you need to progress as a trader and then stay focused on the development of those skills, instead of the money, which is merely a by-product of your skills.

3. Learning how to adapt yourself to respond to fundamental changes in market conditions more readily.

4. Identifying the amount of risk you are comfortable with— your "risk comfort level"—and then learn how to expand it in a way that is consistent with your ability to maintain an objective perspective of market activity.

5. Learning how to execute your trades immediately upon your perception of an opportunity.

6. Learning how to let the market tell you how much is enough, instead of assessing the potential from your personal value system of how much is enough.

7. Learning how to structure your beliefs to control your perception of market movement.

8. Learning how to achieve and maintain a state of objectivity.

9. Learning how to recognize "true" intuitive information and then learning how to act on it consistently.

HOW IS THIS DIFFERENT FROM A TRADING SYSTEM?

Trading systems give us a way to define, quantify, and categorize market behavior. Since the markets offer traders a seemingly infinite combination of behaviors, all with their corresponding opportunities and risks, it is easy to understand how our minds can become overwhelmed. Trading systems limit the scope of market behavior, and therefore make this activity a little easier for our minds to manage. They also give us direction and suggestions about what to do in a given market situation. Without them traders could easily feel as if they are floating aimlessly in an endless sea of possibilities and opportunities with no land in sight.

Since trading systems define opportunity and offer suggestions, following these suggestions can lead to the development of skills, even though as suggestions they merely point the way for your awareness to be directed. A true skill not only points the way, but almost automatically begins to direct awareness as well. And a thinking methodology controls the selection of which skills should be used and when.

I do not offer a trading system in this book. It's more a means of interfacing a trading system with the mind's psychological structure. If a trading system provides awareness of market signals, and suggests behaviors appropriate for any given market situation, then the thinking methodology I will share with you teaches skills and processes of skill application.

Having the skills necessary to consciously manipulate one's psychological environment is essential for the trader who recognizes how ineffectual a trading system can suddenly become whenever a tense situation demands a split-second decision.

Most everyone reading a book of this nature would consider himself as successful to one degree or another, either through trial and error, or the rigorous application of some proven formula, through which each has learned—intentionally or not—skills or methodologies of thought to achieve this success.

In any case, we all have a natural tendency not only to want to achieve success in something, but also to apply the principles of success that work very well in one situation to practically everything else. It often doesn't occur to us that some environments may require very different psychological resources to achieve success.

Suppose, for example, that you arbitrarily tried to apply a certain thought system of success to trading futures or stocks without first investigating the usefulness or validity of that system in relationship to the actual conditions as they exist in the markets. More than likely, you would be doomed to failure before you even started.

Obviously people don't consciously start trading with the belief that they don't have the right resources or that they're going to fail. In fact, it is just the opposite. Because most traders come from or still enjoy very successful careers outside of trading, they have a great deal of confidence in their ability to extend this success in the trading environment. This unfounded confidence, coupled with the way the markets distort a person's concept of reward in relationship to time and effort expended, will cause the trader to form some very unrealistic expectations about the kind of results he should achieve.

Believing that trading is easy is the reason for the unrealistic expectations. And they are probably the single biggest reason why most
traders never make it beyond the initial levels of development before
they lose all their money.

Starting out believing that trading is easy is a psychological trap
that entices almost all traders. But it isn't too difficult to understand
why, when you examine the dynamics of the process of how we set
up a standard of performance for ourselves by which to gauge our
progress. There are four basic components that make up a person's
standard of performance or expectations for results.

First is our basic concept of time; most people believe that it is
limited, passing nonstop and will eventually run out. Second is our
concept of effort—our supply of personal energy is not inexhaustible;
it runs out, we tire, and we may even become ill if we don't rest
properly. The third is our concept of expertise—the number of skills
we have learned and our degree of proficiency in using these skills; it
usually takes a great deal of time and energy to acquire expertise.

Now one of the primary ways we learn to value ourselves is based
on our belief about how much work we do and the amount of time
it takes to do it. Which brings us to the fourth component in the
equation: reward. To determine the amount of reward we should
receive, we will make an assessment about how hard or easy a job is
by determining how much effort (personal energy) we will need to
expend and to assess how long the job will take (using up our limited
time), so we can then determine how much we should be compen-
sated. It is like our own personal supply and demand formula for our
time and energy.

Now I am going to put all this together to demonstrate how
trading distorts all these components in a way that allows someone
to believe that trading is easy. First, to function in the market environment requires very little if any physical effort, especially for the
off-the-floor trader. Second, time is not a relevant factor because a
trader can be stunned with thousands of dollars in profits in a
matter of moments. Conceivably, you could put on a trade, never
have the market go against your position, and be rewarded at levels
far beyond your expectations of what is possible. A person can't help
but make the association between the speed at which something like
this could happen and how easy it must be because there was no
physical effort required.

Most people don't have to experience this personally to make the erroneous assumption that trading is easy. They will just naturally do it the first time they experience market action. They will assume that they would have been a buyer at some low point and held on to liquidate the trade for a profit. Even if it's just for a couple of ticks, invariably they will multiply those ticks by several contracts to come up with these mental windfall profits for themselves. These profits could represent an exotic trip, a dream car, or thoughts of financial independence. Then they will compare how long and how hard they normally have to work to get the same amount of money, and what will result is a completely erroneous conclusion that trading is easy.

The problem is that it is almost impossible for the beginning trader to make a reasonable assessment of the level of expertise that is required to function in the trading environment, like learning to limit oneself in an unlimited environment, when possibly for the first time in the trader's life he has the freedom to express himself creatively without any social constraints, or the amount of the time it takes to acquire this expertise, especially when it looks as if the profits should just roll in so easily and so fast. These kinds of assumptions will blind the trader to the true nature of the endeavor. Time is certainly a factor in learning to perceive opportunity or learning how to execute one's trades flawlessly. Both these skills could take a great deal of time to learn. However, neither time nor effort is a factor in relationship to the potential for reward.

So what happens when we don't live up to our own expectations?—especially, when most everyone starts their trading career thinking it's a piece of cake and that they're only moments away from fulfilling their financial dreams? Regardless of how long it may take any individual to admit that he's not making it, the experience is painful and invariably generates feelings of inadequacy, guilt, and even shame. When one fails, especially when the expectations for success are so high, it will create three major psychological obstacles that have to be overcome before any measure of success will be realized.

First, you will need to learn how to release yourself from any feelings of inadequacy, guilt, or shame. Second, you will need to learn how to identify and repair the residual psychological damage caused by the emotionally painful experiences because painful experiences have the potential to generate fear. Finally, you will need to undo any inappropriate trading habits and learn the appropriate skills that will help you eventually to accumulate the wealth you desire from trading.

For many, what I have outlined may seem like an overwhelming task, and I'm not going to downplay it in the slightest. Even if you haven't as yet subjected yourself to any emotional trauma, just learning the appropriate skills will be no easy task. However, you should keep in mind that the rewards can be astronomical. Would any other endeavor having the unlimited potential of trading in futures or stocks be easy?

As you proceed through this book, it is very important to keep in mind that neither I nor anyone else can deny what you consider to be the structure of reality—even though what I hold to be true and what you hold to be true may differ by a wide margin. Force, violence, or even torture will not cause you or anyone else to give up your beliefs if you don't want to. However, if what I offer will produce a result you desire, then you may be quite willing to suspend, at least temporarily, what you hold to be true and see if what works for me will also work for you.

The fire-walkers I mentioned earlier demonstrated how a thinking methodology could suspend their belief that walking on a bed of hot coals would severely damage their feet—even though they had learned early in their lives the dangers and pain of intense heat. Perhaps you too can suspend some of your beliefs about what makes trading successful. You could find out how your own early training—before you ever considered becoming a trader—may have produced contradictory attitudes and beliefs that cancel all good intentions and optimistic trading, and thus lead to failure.

Understandably, before you even consider the possibility of changing some of your innermost beliefs, you will certainly want to know not only how the process of altering beliefs works but also what benefits it will have for you as a trader.

Like all traders, you have probably read repeatedly what it takes to be successful at trading: "Trade with the trend," "Cut your losses and let your profits run," "Money management is the key," and so on. As true as these adages are, they are too vague to give you a clear understandable connection between the application of these principles and their benefits: a positive and successful trading experience. If you will recall, I listed resistance to accepting a loss among the most common trading errors. If you have ever experienced such resistance, you have probably also encountered the following thought: "How do I accept small losses when what I want to do is make money, and I feel like a failure every time I lose."

Your helplessness in such a situation and the disastrous consequences for your finances are at the essence of this discussion. If, for example, you can change what losses mean to you and how you represent them mentally, then to whatever degree you can accomplish this, you will be releasing yourself from the stress and anxiety experienced when you have to acknowledge any given trade is a loser and take the appropriate action.

The few individuals who have achieved astronomical success in trading at some point learned to stop trying to conquer the markets or make them conform to their expectations or mental limitations. At some point in their trading careers, they understood the psychological implications of an event that is never ending, that begins only when one decides to participate, that ends only when one has had enough, and behaves without the slightest regard for individual survival. Eventually they adapted to these unusual and demanding psychological conditions by changing their perspective, although, as I have already pointed out from my experiences, the process of change usually isn't the result of making a conscious choice to take a step-by-step approach, as this book is designed to give you.

In our everyday lives it is much easier to control the external environment to satisfy our desires. What I mean is, if something has to change to get what we want, we will find it much easier to change the external conditions to suit our needs before we attempt to change our mental perspective. Changing ourselves would seem like the absolute last resort as a solution to any problem. So, why would you consciously go about the task of learning how to change yourself from the inside? I have three reasons for you.

First, because you decide to learn new skills or ways of expressing yourself. Second, because you may have any number of beliefs acting as resistance in the acquisition of the new skills you are attempting to learn. The third I will get to in a moment.

Right now I want to give you an example to illustrate these first two points. A client of mine lost an uncle that he was very close to while he was still a child. His uncle was very much of a father figure to him, where his own father was not. The uncle died of a heart attack at a young age while doing some very strenuous exercise. Because of this experience my client grew up believing he would also die of a heart attack, if he exercised too strenuously.

What would have been just normal heart pounding, to anyone else, after working up a sweat, he would perceive as the beginning of a heart attack. He would start to hyperventilate and stop doing whatever he was doing. Obviously, his belief about dying was very limiting. As a result, he never participated in any sports as a child or well into his adult life.

Well, by the time he was in his late thirties, he decided that he was not going to die prematurely of a heart attack like his uncle. Actually he didn't make this decision until after he passed the age in which his uncle had died. (His uncle's age at the time of his death was the age at which my client thought that he would also die.) When it didn't happen, he gave up the whole notion. Deciding to build up his stamina, he asked me for some tips on how to become a runner, since he knew I had been running for years. In a sense running was a new skill for him and definitely a new way of expressing himself. So we went running together. Of course, what he found out was that he couldn't run. Not that he couldn't take the steps in the fashion of a runner; it is just that every time his heart rate started to climb, he would stop dead in his tracks, even though his intent was to keep on going. His beliefs about dying from exercise still had a great deal of power in his mental environment. This belief acted as resistance, working against his conscious intent to run. Consciously, he was giving his body instructions to keep on going; his conflicting belief, however, was saying, "No way, pal; you're staying right here until your heart rate goes down." In this situation it was very easy to determine what component of his mental system had more power over his behavior.

The third reason why you would want to learn to change from the inside instead of forcing the environment to conform to your psychological makeup relates strictly to trading. The markets are just too big for one person or even a group of individuals to prevail for long. That is, if you don't have the financial power to move prices in your direction, then you are going to have to learn how to flow with and constantly adapt to the outer conditions.

The choice is you can either adapt or continue to experience some very painful lessons. A quick hint: the intensity of your emotional discomfort and pain you experience as a trader is an excellent indication of how much you will have to change to trade without fear and be consistently successful.

You might ask, "Why consider the market from a psychological perspective at all? Doesn't the market behave as it does regardless of what a single individual thinks or feels about it?"

My answer is this: "The market behaves as it does because of the interactions of hundreds of thousands of people. And since all these individuals are members of the human race, regardless of national origin, religious conviction, or what have you, they will all have one thing in common—the psychological structure of the human mind." This psychological structure behaves in certain highly predictable ways whenever it encounters stress or split-second decisions. In the market, the fear of losing one's fortune is every bit as intense as the fear of losing one's life from an attack by a wild animal.

However, even though we all participate collectively, the market is not the same for all of us. Every move the market makes has a different meaning and impact on each of us as individuals. And every trader's experience of this movement is the result of his individual mental process of inputting environmental information (perception) and all the unique internal psychological factors that affect his behavior. So, even though two or more traders can agree on what the current price is, they will not be sharing the same experience of how that price is impacting them personally.

The meaning you place on any particular price change is the result of your beliefs. As a trader you constantly have to define what is high and what is low relative to your beliefs about the future. That is the only way you can make money: buy low and sell it back at a higher price (in the future) or sell high and buy it back at a lower price (in the future). As long as prices continue to move, that movement will create opportunities to buy low and sell high or sell high and buy low, and these opportunities are available for all traders. *You create the game in your own mind based on your beliefs, intents, perceptions, and rules.* It is your own unique perspective and no one else's and the secret is, you can and do choose how you perceive events. Even if you are not aware of exactly how to control and change your perception to make other choices available to yourself, you are still choosing, even if it is out of ignorance.

Until you learn the appropriate skills, your success as a trader will be determined by a number of psychological factors that often have little or nothing to do with the markets.

UNSUCCESSFUL TRADERS

There are many reasons why traders are not successful. These reasons can be broken down into three broad categories.

Lack of Skills

The trader is generally not aware that the trading environment is different from all other environments. Trading has the appearance of something that should be easy to do coupled with the possibility of making vast amounts of money in a relatively short period of time.

The trader will thus create some inflated expectations of success. Adherence to these inflated expectations without the appropriate skills equals disappointment which equals pain which equals psychological damage which equals fear. Fear diminishes the trader's ability to be objective, execute his trades, or learn about the fundamental nature of the markets.

Of course, it is possible to make money without the appropriate skills. However, without these skills the trader will invariably lose what he made back to the markets plus more. The result is disappointment, pain, psychological damage, and fear.

People generally don't know how to repair psychological damage and as a result don't know how to release themselves from their fear. To compensate, we learn some very sophisticated ways of covering our fear up. In society we can get by and even be successful with a facade of confidence because people will generally support each other's illusions about themselves. The market, however, has no vested interest in supporting anyone's illusions about himself. If a trader is feeling fearful, he can try to cover it up all he wants but his trading results will readily reflect his true feelings.

Limiting Beliefs

Most people have a whole assortment of beliefs that argue against their success as a trader. Some of these beliefs you may be consciously aware of, most of them you may not be aware of. In any case, you cannot negate their significance in how they will determine and affect your behavior as a trader.

Many traders will try to circumvent confronting these limiting beliefs by becoming an expert market analyst. It doesn't matter how good a market analyst you become; if you don't release yourself from the effects of these beliefs, you won't be successful to the extent these limiting beliefs have power in your mental system. There are many market gurus who can predict market moves with uncanny accuracy but can't make money as a trader. Either they don't know the nature of beliefs and how they affect and determine behavior, or they don't want to confront the issues surrounding these beliefs. You have to want to do it or nothing will happen. And if you choose not to, you will be subjecting yourself to the same recurring cycles of negative experiences again and again until you either decide to work through whatever issues are necessary or lose all your money and have to give it up.

Lack of Self-Discipline

If the type of environmental conditions exist that are beyond your skill level to respond to appropriately (without doing harm to yourself), then you will need to institute some rules and limitations to guide your behavior until you learn how to act in your best interests. When you were a child your parents didn't let you cross the street by yourself because the consequences of your inability to cross safely might have precluded your getting a second chance. When you were able to make the appropriate distinctions about the nature of traffic, your parents trusted you enough to cross the street on your own.

Until they trusted you, they always feared the possibility of your getting hit by a car. As a result of their fear, they restricted your freedom of movement, regardless of the opportunities that may have existed for you across the street. Your interaction with the trading environment works the same way. The difference is that no one is stopping you from standing in the middle of the street (metaphorically) to get hit by a truck. You are the only one who can stop yourself. After you have been hit once or twice, it might not be so easy to cross the street, regardless of how good the opportunities look on the other side.

What makes it even more difficult (continuing with the traffic metaphor) to step out into the street is when you further realize that the cars and trucks can come at you in a seemingly random fashion. All of a sudden you're lying on the street not even knowing what hit you because you thought you were being careful.

PART II

The Nature of the Trading Environment from a Psychological Perspective

In Chapters 1 and 2 the material presented outlined some of the difficulties of trading. In the next six chapters, I will get much more specific by explaining the characteristics of the market environment from the psychological perspective of the individual trader. From this perspective it will become clear to you how the market environment is much different from the cultural environment you learned to function within. This will confront you with some very unusual psychological challenges.

My primary objective is for you to understand clearly why any degree of success as a trader is so elusive, attained by so few, and why you may need to change some deeply ingrained cultural attitudes and beliefs to function successfully in the trading environment.

CHAPTER 3

The Market
Is Always Right

If all trading stopped at any particular price, what would this last posted price represent? At the most fundamental level, this last price (or any current price) would represent the consensus belief about value, relative to the future, of all the traders who are in the market in that moment. The current price is a direct reflection of the beliefs of all the traders who choose to act as a force on prices by putting on a trade. So, when there are two traders, one wanting to buy and one wanting to sell at a price and do so, they have made a trade, and they have also made a market.

All that is needed to make the market right are two traders willing to trade at a price. Regardless of the criteria they used to determine value, how rational, irrational, meaningful, or meaningless by your or anyone else's belief system, if two traders are willing to express their belief in future value by making a trade, they have made a market. Unless the trade can be undone, it has to be right by virtue of the fact that it was made.

What you wanted, thought, believed, or expected is of no consequence in the overall scheme of things unless you can trade with enough volume to control the market and move prices in the direction you deem to be correct. To do this, you would personally have to represent a buying or selling force strong enough to absorb all the counteracting buying or selling represented by the traders who didn't happen to agree with you, at any given moment, with enough financial power left over to bid or offer the price where you want it to be.

For an observer of market behavior, each trade that is made and the type of movement it creates in prices can tell you something about the consistency of the market and potential for movement in a direction—if you can discern the meaning and put that meaning within some framework defining opportunity. Price movement creates opportunities to buy low and sell high, or vice versa, if you can perceive what is likely to be high and low relative to some point in the future. Movement in any given direction is equivalent to the amount of force that is being applied to create that movement.

For example, if prices penetrated all-time lows, the fact that you may have believed that they would not do it is meaningless, unless you can personally trade with enough volume to move the price back above the old low. You have to consider that for prices to have penetrated all-time lows, there must have been more traders who believed that the current price was above what they considered to be of value, at least enough to where they believed the all-time low was a selling opportunity or they would not have sold. For prices to follow through and continue to go lower would indicate that there are more traders willing to act on their belief that prices are high and as a result sell than there are traders who are willing to buy at those prices (all-time lows).

What you believed about value and your reasons for believing it may be of highest quality, but if the market doesn't share your belief, it doesn't really matter how "right" you are based on your superior reasoning process or what you believe to be the quality of your information, because prices are going to go in the direction of the greatest force.

The point here is that right and wrong as you may traditionally think of them don't exist in the market environment. Academic credentials, degrees, reputations, even a high I.Q. don't make you right in this environment as they would in society. Traders, acting on their belief in the future by putting on a trade, are the only force that can act on prices to make them move. Movement creates opportunity to make money, and making money is what trading is all about. This is also true for the hedger trading to protect the value of his assets.

Each individual trader will define what market condition represents enough of an opportunity to put on a trade for whatever reason suits him. Regardless of how wrong you think he may be, if the net result of the collective actions of all the traders participating is moving prices against your position, then they're right and you're the one who is losing money.

The market is never wrong in what it does; it just is. Therefore, you as an individual trader interacting with the market—first as an observer to perceive opportunity, then as a participant executing a trade, contributing to the overall market behavior—have to confront an environment where only you can be wrong, and it's never the other way around. As a trader, you have to decide what is more important—being right or making money—because the two are not always compatible or consistent with one another.

CHAPTER 4

There Is
Unlimited Potential for
Profit and Loss

The most effective manner to illustrate the "unlimitedness" of the market environment is to compare it to gambling. With any gambling game you will always know exactly how much you can win or lose each time you play. You decide exactly how much you want to wager, you know exactly how much you can win as well as lose, and you may even know the mathematical odds of either possibility.

This is not the case in market environment. In any particular trade you never really know how far prices will travel from any given point. If you never really know where the market may stop, it is very easy to believe there are no limits to how much you can make on any given trade.

From a psychological perspective this characteristic will allow you to indulge yourself in the illusion that each trade has the potential of fulfilling your wildest dream of financial independence. Based on the consistency of market participants (ratio between buyers and sellers) and their potential to act as a force great enough to move prices in your direction, the possibility of having your dreams fulfilled may not even remotely exist. However, if you believe it does, then you will have the tendency to gather only the kind of market information that will confirm and reinforce your belief, all the while denying vital information that may be telling you the best opportunity is in the opposite direction.

If you are in a losing trade, the market could be moving farther and farther away from your entry point, increasing your potential loss by the moment. While this is happening, however, you may only be able to imagine it coming back in your favor, instead of confronting the possibility of the market continuing against your position. This type of thought process will continue until the sheer magnitude of the loss overwhelms you, and the possibility of the loss increasing is suddenly more pertinent than the possibility of the market coming back. You finally exit the trade never intending or ever imagining you could have allowed yourself to take such a large loss.

From a psychological perspective, the possibility for unlimited profits, happiness, power, and so on, whatever it means to you when you imagine making all the money you ever wanted to make, can be extremely dangerous. The possibility may in fact exist, but how realistic it is in any given trade is another matter.

There are several psychological factors that go into being able to assess accurately the market's potential for movement in any given direction. One of them is releasing yourself from the notion that each trade has the potential to fulfill all your dreams. At the very least this illusion will be a major obstacle keeping you from learning how to perceive market action from an objective perspective. Otherwise, if you continually filter market information in such a way as to confirm this belief, learning to be objective won't be a concern because you probably won't have any money left to trade with.

CHAPTER 5

Prices Are in Perpetual Motion with No Defined Beginning or Ending

The markets are always in motion; they never stop, only pause. As long as there are traders who, for whatever reasons, are willing to buy higher than the last price and, as a result, bid the price up, or traders willing to sell for less than the last price and offer the market lower, prices will remain in perpetual motion. Even when the markets are closed, prices are theoretically in motion. For example, what price traders may be willing to buy or sell at on the opening the next day does not have to be at the price level the market closed at the previous day.

What are usually thought of as three simple decisions of enter, hold, or liquidate a trade become a perpetual process of deciding how much is enough from both a profit and a loss perspective. If you are in a profitable trade, is there ever enough? Greed stems from a belief that there is never enough or there won't be enough. In an unlimited environment that is in perpetual motion, isn't there always the possibility of getting more? The appetite of true greed can never be satisfied; it will always leave the greedy ones with a feeling of lacking regardless of how much they have acquired. If you are in a losing trade, you won't want it to exist because it represents failure, so you can just act as if it doesn't, by convincing yourself that you are in a winning trade that hasn't gone in your favor yet.

The "how much is enough" question can be answered in an infinite number of ways relative to your beliefs on the value of money, what you need it for, how important it is, can you really risk it, how secure do you feel, and what is enough today may not be enough tomorrow because of other factors in your life—all relative questions that have no definitive answers and change with the changing environmental conditions. Having to confront these personal issues as a trader will only contaminate your observations of market movement because they have nothing to do with market direction and the potential or lack of potential of any particular market move. This is why successful traders have always stated emphatically, "Only trade with money you can afford to lose," meaning money that has little or no value in your life. The less meaning the money has, the less potential there is for your personal "how much is enough" issues to contaminate your perception of market movement.

Thus, if you allow it, the market can always tempt you into thinking there may be more to be had in a winning trade and always give you something to hang on to in order to justify your hope that it will come back and make you whole, if you are in a losing trade. Succumbing to either one of these temptations subjects you to the possibility of some very negative and painful consequences.

The market environment is also unstructured in such a way that, from a psychological perspective, there is no beginning and there is no ending. What I mean by this statement (before you think that it's not true, the market opens and closes at a specified time every day) is that from the perspective of the individual trader, the game only begins when you decide to enter and ends only when you decide to exit irrespective of market openings and closings.

You have the freedom to structure the game inside your mind in any particular way you please. You can get in whenever you want for whatever reasons are good enough to justify your actions. You can get out whenever you want. In fact the game only ends when you have decided that you've had enough and take the appropriate action to end it. The psychological implications to the individual confronting these conditions are staggering.

Entering a trade will involve all your beliefs about opportunity in relationship to risk, missing out, needing a sure thing, and not being wrong. Exiting a trade will involve all your beliefs about loss, greed, failure, and control.

Considering the unlimited potential for profit, entering the market will be much easier for most traders than will be getting out. This is because exiting the trade will require that you confront your beliefs about greed, loss, and failure in relationship to the constant temptation of the possibility for unlimited profits.

These individual psychological issues are completely independent of objective market action. And even more significant, as I will explain in Part III, your beliefs about loss, being wrong, failure, and control will operate independently of your conscious intent. For example, think of the last time you perceived an opportunity to profit and the fear of being wrong, or losing, and so on, immobilized you, keeping you from putting on the trade.

To the extent that these issues exist as a component of your mental environment, they will determine the effect they have on your perception of market activity, the decisions you make, and your ability to act on what you decide.

However, one of the most significant and potentially damaging factors related to this no beginning and no ending characteristic of the market environment is that it allows you to be a passive loser. The best way to illustrate this concept is to compare the markets with any form of gambling games. For example, with blackjack, horse racing, or craps the player has to make a conscious choice to play and decide before the event exactly how much he will wager. The event begins and ends according to the rules of the game, and the risk of loss is limited to the size of the wager.

Each new event is a fresh start, where the odds of winning may be determined by mathematical probabilities and the rules of the game automatically take the player out after each event. When the game ends, the player knows exactly what the outcome is and then must make a conscious decision to participate again. Therefore, the structure of the game forces the player to be an active loser. To subject himself to the possibility of losing any more money than he has already lost requires that he place a wager for a specified amount. He has to actively participate to lose and do nothing to stop losing. Obviously, if the player does nothing, he will not be subjecting his assets to the possibility of loss.

If the player is losing consistently, he will need to confront his beliefs about loss and failure to quit playing altogether. This could be difficult because he can always rationalize that, based on the odds, he is bound to win eventually and that he can always quit after the next game. But he does not need his own mental structure to end any particular game because it's automatic.

This is very much different from the market environment where you can be a passive loser. Once you put on a trade, you have to actively participate to end your losses. You don't need to do anything to continue to lose, and the market could go against your position indefinitely. If for any reason you choose not to act or can't act, you could lose everything you own and more. Depending on the size of your position and the volatility of the market, this could happen very quickly. The only way out is to confront your personal issues about greed, loss, and failure. What specific issues or combination of them come into play in each trade will depend on whether you are in a winning or losing position.

Since, all of us seem instinctively to avoid confronting any issue that could cause pain, such as getting out of a winning trade too soon or having to admit we were wrong to get out of a loser, the easiest way out of a situation like this is to convince ourselves (indulge ourselves in the illusion) we are in a winning trade that will never end or gather all the evidence possible to suggest that we really aren't in a losing trade. Therefore, in either case we will have no reason to confront the forces inside of us that keep us from objectively perceiving what the market is telling us about the possibilities and potential for profit in any given moment.

The markets make it extremely easy for you not to have to confront these very tough psychological issues. For example, if you focus your attention on price movement at the tick-by-tick level, the market can graphically display billions of combinations of behavior characteristics and price patterns to get from one point to the next. It is very easy to use this type of information to support any belief, rationalization, justification, distortion, or illusion you need to want to have about where it is going in the future.

Most traders will attempt to simplify price movement by thinking the price can only do three things. Go up, go down, or stay basically the same. Some traders may even carry this distorted logic to the point where they believe there is a 50/50 probability for success in any give trade. This of course couldn't be further from the truth. For example, let's say that prices stayed within a 10-tick trading range for an entire trading session, if you take into account each tick, how many price patterns is it possible for the market to display going from the top to bottom of the range and then back again? I'm not a statistician, but I'm sure it's at least millions. To illustrate this a little further, if point A is the bottom of the range, prices could have changed up one tick, down two, up one, down three, up two, down one, up one, down two, up three, down one, up two, down one, up one, down one, up two, down one, up three, down one, up two, down one, up three, down one, up one, down one, up two, down one, up three to point B, ten ticks up from point A. This is obviously a very shortened version of the way prices usually move, but it does represent one pattern out of millions of possible pattern combinations, and each pattern you identify can repeat itself at some point in the future.

If you are a buyer at point A, what are the odds the price will stay above your entry point? What are the odds that the price will be above or significantly above your entry point tomorrow or the next day without having gone below your entry point first, by two ticks, five ticks, or ten ticks, before it goes back up again above your entry point? Once prices go below your entry point, what are the odds they never go above your entry point? What are the odds they never go below? To answer these questions, you would have to know a great deal about the consistency of the market and its potential to behave in certain ways. In any case, relative to most traders' emotional disposition to deal with this kind of movement and within the context that most people think of as 50/50 odds, it definitely doesn't apply in the markets.

To illustrate another point, if you got short halfway between points A and B, which ticks would you have the tendency to place greater weight on in terms of market information? The down ticks naturally. They confirm what you believe and the up ticks don't. Yet each in relationship to one another can tell you something about the consistency of the market and its potential to move in any given direction. How can you begin to assess that potential accurately if you place a greater significance specifically on the information that confirms what you want or believe? In effect, you would be using the information to suit your hopes, dreams, wishes, and desires instead of perceiving it in a manner to assess the market's actual potential to do any of the foregoing.

Thus, what you have in the market environment is a deadly combination of the market forcing you to confront difficult personal issues to survive, an event that produces information in a wide variety of forms that can be used to support any illusion, distortion, or expectation, therefore, making it easy to avoid confronting these potentially painful issues. Furthermore the event continues on until you come to terms with whatever is inside of you to end it. Unless your brokerage firm liquidates your position, you are the only one who can make it stop.

Among many other factors, to become a consistently successful trader your objective has to be to learn how to let the market tell you what it may do next and how much is enough. This is extremely difficult when you consider there is absolutely no relationship between what the market may do next and your personal belief system on what it means to lose, what it means to be wrong, greed (fear founded in a belief there will never be enough), and revenge.

I can anticipate a lot of readers saying to themselves "I can understand the loss, being wrong, and greed issues, but where does revenge come into this?" This can best be illustrated by going back to the gambling game example. In a gambling game you can only lose what you decide to risk. You bet the money and it's difficult not to accept the responsibility for any losses. As a trader, however, you could easily lose far more than you intended to risk, based on your inability to perceive the possible or your inability to execute a trade to get out of your position, or a combination of both.

You may have been willing to take responsibility for what you originally intended to risk on a trade (although most traders are not willing to take this responsibility, which I will demonstrate further on); however, it might not be so easy to take responsibility for losing more than what you intended to risk. This is where the revenge factor comes into play. If you don't take responsibility for what you lost, then who or what can you blame—the markets, of course. The markets took your money. If the markets took from you more than you originally intended to risk, then you will likely feel compelled to get it back.

For example, is a 10-tick profit enough in the trade you are currently in if you lost 20 in the last trade? The market may be giving the objective observer a very clear indication that where the price is now is all that is left in the move and the highest probability for success is to take profits now. If you lost 20 ticks in the last trade and you only intended to risk 5 and the market is now offering you 10, are you going to take it. If you believe in "getting back," 10 won't be enough regardless of what the market is doing or telling you. You will need at least 15 and preferably 20 to make you whole.

Your last trade obviously has nothing to do with the potential that exists in the market at any given moment. When you feel compelled to get back, it puts you in an adversary relationship with the market. The market becomes your opponent, it is you against it, instead of being in harmony with it. The market can't take anything away from you that you don't allow; if you lost money or lost more than you intended to risk, you gave your money to other traders. Ultimately, however, revenge creates an adversary relationship with yourself. If you're the one who gives your money to the market, you are also the one who gives yourself money out of the market. If you are angry with yourself for letting the last trade get so out of hand, whatever the market is offering you "now" in terms of an opportunity won't be enough. From a psychological perspective, you won't take the opportunity for a profit or otherwise because you haven't accepted the last trade as being all right. In effect, you will be denying yourself the current or next opportunity to punish yourself for the past mistake. In reality you can't get back at the market, and a belief in revenge only allows you to get back at yourself.

There is a direct correlation between your ability to let the market tell you what it is likely to do next and the degree to which you have released yourself from the negative effects of any beliefs about losing, being wrong, and revenge on the markets. Not being aware of this relationship, most traders will continue to observe the market from a contaminated perspective until they either make the association through trial and error or become aware of this relationship through a book such as this. In any case, by the time those who figure it out do so, they have usually subjected themselves to so much psychological damage that it adds a much more difficult dimension to the process of becoming successful.

This is the principal reason why this book had to address the areas of personal transformation in such depth: you need to know if there is any damage, how to identify it, and most important, how to release yourself from it.

CHAPTER 6

The Market Is an Unstructured Environment

Unlike structured social activities that have defined beginnings and endings and rigid rules to guide your behavior, the market environment is more like a river constantly flowing, with no beginning or ending with almost no structure. Once you jump in the river, it can change directions at any moment. It may have been flowing north when you jumped in; however, without any notice, it can start flowing south. It's unstructured to the point where you make up all your own rules to play by, with a great deal of latitude to do so.

You will have to decide if and when you're going to jump in and with how much force. If you are already in, you have the option of increasing the force you apply at any time or of decreasing it. There are no rules preventing you from jumping out at any moment to change your intended direction to flow with the market, or you can jump out and stay out, and the market just keeps on flowing.

In an unstructured and unlimited environment, it is essential that you establish rules to guide your behavior. You will need to create definition and give yourself direction. Otherwise, you will feel overwhelmed with too many possibilities. Without these rules one of the most likely possibilities is that you will create devastating losses for yourself. The big psychological problem here is, if you make up and have to play by your own rules, you also have to take total and complete responsibility for your actions as well as the outcome of your actions. The degree to which you do assume responsibility is the same degree to which you can't shift it to the market and be its victim.

The typical trader will do most anything to avoid creating definition and rules because he does not want to take responsibility for the results of his trading. If he knows exactly what he is going to do and under what conditions, then he would have something by which to measure his performance, thus making himself accountable to himself. This is exactly what most traders don't want to do, preferring instead to keep their relationship with the market somewhat mysterious.

This creates a real psychological paradox for traders, because the only way to learn how to trade effectively is to make oneself accountable by creating structure; but, with accountability comes responsibility. The typical trader desperately wants to make money, but he has to do it in a way where there is no direct connection between what he does and the outcome that it produces, thereby avoiding responsibility if things don't turn out satisfactorily.

To develop a plan, you have to anticipate events to some extent relative to the depth of your plan. When you plan your trades in advance, you are putting your vision of the future and creative abilities on the line, so to speak, and making yourself accountable to yourself. Your plan either works or it doesn't; you either have the ability to execute your plan or you don't. In any case, it is your plan and your ability to follow it and, therefore, it is difficult to shift responsibility and lay the blame somewhere else if things don't work out.

Now, when a trader doesn't understand market behavior well enough to know what he is going to do and under what market conditions he is going to do it—but if at the same time, he is very attracted to the action and the opportunities he knows exist and if he is also impatient with the learning process—his impatience and attraction will make him feel compelled to do something, even if he doesn't know what he should do. How do you think the typical trader will resolve this dilemma? He will play follow the leader, rationalizing that everybody else is doing something and, furthermore, all these people waving their hands and screaming can't be as afraid and unknowing as himself, so they must know what they are doing or at least they know more than him. If he does what they do, or better yet, identifies the most successful trader and does what that trader does, then he too can make money.

This type of rationale creates a herd mentality (extremely prevalent on the floor of the exchanges), where most everyone is looking for direction, assuming everyone else must know something they don't, otherwise why would they be doing anything. In a group, this collective mentality is very volatile, where one key trader can start an endless series of chain reactions where everyone mirrors everyone else, all assuming that the other guy must have some rational reason for doing what he is doing.

In fact, I wouldn't even describe what goes on down on the trading floor as follow the leader. It is actually better described as "follow the follower," because most traders don't know what the leader is doing or who the leader may be at any given moment. Therefore, the group's behavior is like these endless waves of back and forth movement, where the traders closest to the leaders (the leaders being those who know exactly what they want to do and why they want to do it) will have the first opportunity to get on the bandwagon at the best price and those next closest have diminished opportunities and so on down the line until you get to the least skilled trader, who doesn't have much of a chance at all. When there is no leadership in the market, the prices usually drift back and forth in a small range until someone who knows what he is doing comes into the market.

If the prices have made any significant move during or at the end of the trading day, all the crowd followers get together to find any reason or rationale that might explain their (the market's) behavior and put it into some understandable context. Basically, what they come up with is a consensus reason for the market's behavior that day. However, the leaders (those traders who take responsibility for their trades and know exactly why they did what they did) do not feel compelled to talk to anyone and usually don't. The typical crowd follower feels compelled to find reasons outside of himself because these reasons don't exist inside of himself and he doesn't want to think he is irrational and acts randomly.

For the crowd follower, trading this way serves many functions. It keeps his relationship with the market mysterious. If he makes money, he must have done something right. If he loses money, he can blame the market, which is obviously very acceptable behavior among traders, since so many of them do it. The rational or logical explanation for the individual's part in the collective behavior will be decided on later (after the fact) by the consensus opinion of the group. This way he can maintain an illusion of being rational and responsible and whatever happened to him also happened to a lot of other traders, so at least he knows he is not alone, which then creates a sense of comradeship among competitors.

Outside of the world of trading, most people think that traders are rugged individualists, associating them with the characteristics of the entrepreneurial types, like being decisive and persevering. Most outside people would be shocked to learn that except for a small minority of successful traders, the rest fall into a group that, at any given moment, have no idea about what they are going to do next or know why they are even doing what they are doing. If you asked them to tell you specifically how they make money or lose money, they couldn't tell you. In addition, as a group, traders (except for the leaders) are indecisive and impatient to an extreme. It isn't too difficult to determine why, if you consider that under normal conditions, the frame of mind of the average trader is one notch away from unrestrained terror. Getting organized and creating structure is one obvious solution to the many psychological problems the typical trader heaps on himself. But that would also force him to cross that psychological boundary line into the realm of accountability and responsibility.

Besides the outright refusal to plan trades, most traders go to great lengths to put as much psychological distance as possible between what they do and the outcome of their actions. I know many traders who can do extremely good market analysis on their own but still seek opinions of other traders on what to do and then take those trades instead of their own, simply because they don't want to take responsibility if the trade doesn't work out. And, more often than not, sticking with their own analysis would have produced far better results.

There are many floor traders who trade hundreds of contracts a day, and although they have to record each trade on a trading card, they will not keep an accurate account of their net trading position, claiming they get too busy or that they added wrong. At the end of the day, they count their cards with intense anxiety, hoping or praying to whatever unseen forces that they are flat (not carrying a net long or short position).

Obviously, if they were that concerned, the simple solution to their problem would be to trade only at a volume level where they can always keep track of where they are at and if they lose track to stop trading until they get a correct count. But they wouldn't want to do that because, if they kept track of their position, then they would have to take the responsibility for what they end up with. What if they inadvertently end up with a net long position at the end of the day and the market opens several ticks higher the next morning? The unseen market forces have thus blessed these traders with a winning position, or conversely if the market opens lower, they can always find someone or something to blame for their bad fortune. Maybe their lucky tie was sent to the dry cleaners by mistake or they hit three red lights in a row on the way to the exchange. Any reason or excuse to shift responsibility will do. These reasons can range from the most eloquent academic jargon to the most superstitious beliefs, but in essence, they all focus blame outside of oneself for unsatisfactory results.

In an unlimited environment, the less structure you create for yourself, the less accountable you are, the more easily you will be swept along by the force of events, and the less control you seem to have over your life. However, having less structure has the benefit of shifting the responsibility for the events in your life to other unidentified forces. This is precisely why so many traders have such a strong belief in superstitions. If a person refuses to make any connection between his thoughts, intents, skills, and results, then it is very easy to associate one's success or failure to something like the tie one had on that day or inadvertently making some gesture and then finding oneself in a losing trade and associating the gesture with the loss.

I have a personal story to illustrate a typical superstitious belief that traders have. One morning I went into the men's bathroom at the Chicago Mercantile Exchange, and as I approached the only urinal not in use, a floor trader using the urinal next to the one I was about to use turned his head, looked at me, and said in a very cautious tone, "Don't use that one, you can wait for mine, I'll be done in a second." I gave him a puzzled look, and he then pointed to a penny that was at the bottom of the urinal. I gave him another puzzled look because I didn't have the slightest idea about what he was trying to communicate to me. As I proceeded to use the urinal with the penny in it, he turned with a nervous expression on his face and strode away from me as quickly as he could.

Later on that day, I told one of my floor trader clients about this experience and asked if he knew what was going on. He said certainly, that it was very common knowledge that money at the bottom of a urinal is a bad omen and *certainly* something to be avoided. After I thought about it for a moment, I wondered what would happen if I went through the entire exchange and put pennies in all the urinals.

This story illustrates how the typical trader is caught in a psychological trap of refusing to plan and create structure for his trading activity, so that he can avoid taking responsibility for his results. And by doing so, he is subjecting himself to being tossed around by the whims of the crowd, at the mercy of his own unrestrained impulses, finding himself in winning and losing positions, not knowing why or what to do next. This trap is extremely negative because it creates a potentially damaging psychological condition I call random winning and random losing. If you can't define your own behavior and that of the markets, you can't learn how to repeat your wins or prevent your losses.

When you win it is so pleasurable, it creates a need to repeat it and compels you to try again. When you follow the crowd (instead of anticipating the crowd, which would take planning) or trade off news items, tips, or isolated signals from technical systems, the anticipation of the next attempt to win automatically produces fear and anxiety.

Why? Because, you can't define the market conditions or the decision-making process that produced the last win, and so you can't assure yourself of the next.

If you don't know what you did to win the last time, you obviously don't know what to do to keep from losing this time. The end result is intense anxiety, frustration, confusion, and fear. You feel out of control, experiencing a sense of powerlessness as you are swept along by the ensuing events and wondering what is the market going to do to you today.

Consider that the markets can't do anything to any trader who completely trusts himself to act appropriately, in his best interests, under all market conditions. And before people can trust themselves in this manner, they would first have to define all those conditions and be able to recognize them.

Understandably, taking responsibility is something that is extremely difficult to do. We don't live in a society that has a highly evolved concept of the growth process, and as a result, we learn to become very intolerant of "mistakes." I say this because we are basically taught as children and, therefore, in turn teach our children through our ridicule of them that mistakes are something that diminish one as a person. Ridicule does not enhance a child's willingness to accept responsibility, and if he doesn't, the typical parent will then criticize the child for being irresponsible.

Taking responsibility is a function of self-acceptance. You can measure this degree of self-acceptance by how positively or negatively you think of yourself when you make what you perceive as a mistake. The more negatively you think of yourself, the greater your tendency to avoid taking responsibility, so you can avoid the pain of your harsh thoughts, thus generating a fear of making mistakes. However, the greater the degree of self-acceptance you have for yourself, the more positive your thoughts will be and the greater the degree of insight you will be able to extract from an experience, instead of generating fear. The more self-accepting you are, the easier it is to learn because you are not trying to avoid certain information.

I don't know of any national prerogative to teach children how to accept themselves in spite of their "shortcomings" as perceived by the adults in their lives. If people had a more accepting attitude about the outcome of their actions, they wouldn't have a need to avoid taking responsibility.

To be successful, the market forces you, as a trader, to be responsible in completely new ways. For example, you can't put on a trade and then release your responsibility to the market to do something for you, like give you money. The market is a fluid, ever-changing event, where at any moment some other trader may decide to jump in with enough force to change the expectations of other traders participating to the point where they reverse their positions and as a result completely negate the potential you believed existed a moment ago, when you put on your trade.

In our everyday lives, objects are very stable, and day-to-day events do not change at anywhere near the rate and frequency that conditions change in the market environment. Relative to the nature of the market environment, all of us take it completely for granted that the buildings, trees, traffic lights, and streets we all know are completely stationary and will be there from one moment to the next. You didn't walk out of your front door this morning to discover the street you live on doesn't look just as it did the previous evening when you walked inside your home. If getting to the office or your place of employment represents an opportunity to make money, you would take it completely for granted that it would be possible to get there in familiar ways.

However, as a potential opportunity to make money comparable to that afforded in the markets, what if the location changed on a moment-to-moment basis, what if the streets also changed their location in relationship to each other, and, furthermore, what if no one cared if you ever found your way there, making you and you alone completely responsible for where you end up?

It just makes sense that to function in the market environment effectively you will need to make yourself accountable. Otherwise, how could you ever learn how to trade, if you allow yourself to be swept into or out of something by forces outside of you and inside of you that you can't identify and don't want to? The market's behavior will seem mysterious because your own behavior is mysterious. You will be in a constant state of confusion, anxiety, and fear because you don't know what to do next—the kind of state of mind that breeds superstition.

Understanding yourself is synonymous with understanding the markets because as a trader you are part of the collective force that moves prices. How could you begin to understand the dynamics of group behavior well enough to extract money from the group, as a result of their behavior, if you don't understand the inner forces that affect your own? When you do understand the inner forces that affect your behavior and take responsibility for what you do and don't do, and what you can or can't do, you will begin to perceive how and why other traders comprising the group behave the way they do.

When you attain some degree of control over yourself, you can then see how other traders are not in control of what happens to them, like blades of grass, all bending to the force of the prevailing wind and constantly being stepped on. You won't be able to see this until you are no longer a blade of grass yourself by evolving beyond the group mentality. Then it becomes much easier to understand the group's behavior, anticipate what they will likely do next, and take advantage of it to the best of your ability. You will understand the group, certainly, to no greater degree than you understand yourself.

Creating definition and rules to make yourself accountable is but a first step on the road to lasting success. You could acknowledge their necessity and establish them, but then find to your dismay, it is extremely difficult to abide by them. In Part III we will examine the interacting mental forces that make it difficult to follow your own rules.

CHAPTER 7

In the Market Environment, Reasons Are Irrelevant

I have titled this chapter "In the Market Environment Reasons Are Irrelevant" in recognition of the traders who believe that if they can ascertain the reasons why the market did what it did, these reasons will help them to determine what the market will do next. To believe this assumes that traders know why they behaved as they did and that the reasons they give for their actions will aid in determining their future behavior.

The reasons traders would give for their actions are irrelevant. Most traders don't know why they did what they did because most traders don't plan their trades, thus eliminating any connection between themselves and the results of their trades. Most traders act spontaneously and impulsively and then ascribe the rationale for their behavior after the fact. Most of these after-the fact reasons are either justifications for what traders did or excuses for what traders didn't do.

Fundamentally people trade to make money. And to make money, traders have to take positions, hold their positions for some length of time, and then exit their positions. When traders enter and exit positions, they act as a force on prices, making them move. When they are observing the market, waiting to enter or holding a position, traders are a potential force that can act on prices at any given moment. If traders planned what they were going to do before they did it, then the reasons they would give for why they act as they do could definitely help other traders to anticipate how prices will be affected by their actions. This, of course, assumes that they will reveal their plans and that they will be telling the truth. There are only a few traders who make money on a consistent basis, and rarely will they reveal their reasons unless it suits their purposes.

In fact, traders who are confident in their ability and know they can have a significant impact on price movement go to great lengths to keep information about their plans away from other traders because that would diminish the possibility of executing these plans. However, this is not to say that after they have taken their positions they won't purposely reveal what they have done to then draw other traders into the same position, forcing them to compete among each other to create price movement in their direction. On the other hand, traders who are not confident about what they want to do will gladly share their trading ideas with anyone who will listen, hoping to get some sort of confirmation that what they are about to do will work. So the after-the-fact reasons they offer for why they acted as they did usually just serve the purpose of easing the pain of what they perceive as their mistakes, which isn't particularly useful information.

What is useful is understanding that traders typically act as a group, very similar to a school of fish or herd of cattle. Individual traders fall into specific groups that tend to perceive the same kind of market conditions as opportunities or disappointments. As a result, they will act in unison to upset the balance of the market, causing the prices to move in predominately one direction. The various groups take positions because they believe they can make money, and they get out because they are either losing money or perceive the possibility of making any more money as diminished in relationship to the perceived risk of losing money. For example, the locals on the floor of the exchanges have the least amount of patience, are the most impulsive, are the most easily disappointed, and consequently have the smallest price objectives and shortest time frame perspectives. As a result, they are the most active and will all be trying to do the same thing at the same time.

Commercials and off-the-floor retail traders are two other groups that have different price objectives and time frame perspectives from each other. Individuals within these groups will also tend to act in unison, upsetting the balance in the market by their degree of participation or lack of participation at any given moment. You can determine what market conditions in which they are most likely to participate, what conditions will confirm their beliefs about the future, and what will disappoint them. Once you learn their unique characteristics, you can anticipate how one or more groups are likely to act and determine how their activity will affect the balance of the market and the potential for price movement.

WHY DO WE TRADE?

Every moment we exist we are interacting with the environment, expressing ourselves in our own unique way, and thus creating our lives by the way we live it. Everything we do in every moment is some form of the way we express ourselves. We express ourselves to fulfill our needs, wants, desires, and goals. Today most individuals can channel their energies to fulfill needs beyond the requirements of food and shelter, but to do so requires money.

Money allows for a system of exchange where we can trade the goods and services created from individuals expressing themselves in highly specialized ways. Money has evolved to become the object of our needs because it represents the means or path by which we can express ourselves as individuals. All behavior is a form of self-expression, and almost any way in which an individual wants to express himself in our society requires money. So at the most fundamental level of cultural existence, money represents freedom of expression.

Individuals expressing themselves in specialized ways create a highly complex system of interdependency. To exchange goods and services, individuals have to agree on the value of those goods and services to make an exchange. I am defining "value" as the relative degree of importance or potential something has in fulfilling a need. The actual price at which goods and services are then exchanged will be determined by the fundamental economic law of supply and demand. In psychological terms, the law of supply and demand is founded in human fear and greed. Both fear and greed will compel people to act or not act depending on their needs in relation to the perceived external conditions. The price for goods and services will be determined by the individual's needs in relationship to their belief in their ability to fulfill those needs. Implied within that belief is their perception of the availability of the goods and services they need.

Greed is founded in a belief in scarcity and insecurity. Both beliefs generate fear. I am defining "greed" as a belief that there will never be enough available to fulfill oneself in combination with a belief that one always needs more to feel secure or satisfied. The perception that these conditions exist either internally or externally will generate a fear that will compel one to act or not act, depending on who controls the supply. The behavior someone displays will be consistent with what they believe they must do to satisfy the deficit. If two or more people have the same fears, they will typically compete among one another for the existing supply.

If the supply of something is limited in relationship to the need, those that are in need will compete for the available supply. They will compete by their willingness to exchange more resources (pay more money) than will someone else who may also be in need. If, however, the supply is great in relationship to the need (demand), there will be no fear of scarcity; consequently, people will conserve their resources (money) by diverting them to other needs or just waiting for the possibility that the price may come down.

Any system of interaction founded in individual fears of lack or scarcity will cause the price of goods and services to fluctuate in relationship to the relative degree of security or insecurity that is being experienced by the collective masses at any given moment. These fluctuating prices create economic risk for all those dependent on others to fulfill a need that they cannot fill themselves. What is risk? Risk is the possibility of a net loss of personal resources (energy, money etc.) in the exchange or pursuit of fulfilling a need. Fluctuating prices also create opportunities for those who are willing to assume the risk created by price movement. As long as there is disagreement between individuals about the value of goods and services, prices will fluctuate, thereby creating opportunities for traders to make money if they will assume the risks.

DEFINITION OF TRADING

I define trading as two parties exchanging something of value to fulfill some need or goal. In the context of the stock or futures markets, participants trade for the sole purpose of accumulating wealth or protecting physical assets from deteriorating in value. In essence, all traders in these markets, whether they are labeled speculators or hedgers, trade to accumulate wealth; it is only a matter of perspective. For the hedger the motivation to protect the value of an asset from economic risk is still to accumulate wealth.

Hedgers will trade for a higher degree of economic certainty by transferring the risk created by changing prices to another willing trader. Typically, it will be the speculator on the other side of the trade willing to assume the risk of changing prices for the opportunity to accumulate wealth from those changes. For example, stock owners will sell their stock because they believe the possibilities for the future appreciation of the stock are either nonexistent or minimal in relationship to their assessment of the risk to keeping it. They may also sell even with expectations of future appreciation if there is a need to liquidate to satisfy other needs. The buyers (the other side of the trade) believe that the stock will appreciate in value. We can assume that the buyer believes this because people trade to accumulate wealth.

Since the goal of a trader is to satisfy a need to accumulate wealth, we can assume that people will not consciously enter into a trade believing they will lose or fail at satisfying their needs. Because all traders have basically the same goals (to win), we can then state that no two traders enter into a trade unless they have opposing beliefs about the future value of whatever is being traded. Keep in mind that the current price of anything is always a reflection of what someone is willing to pay and what someone is willing to sell for in that moment. So, although there must be agreement between two parties for a trade to exist at a price, inherent within the transaction is complete disagreement between buyer and seller on the future value of what they are trading. For example, would I be incorrect in stating that any stock owner will not sell his stock if he believed it had potential for future appreciation. When he sells he has basically given up on the possibilities of future appreciation. Why did the buyer buy? To lose money? To be wrong? No, of course not. The buyer's belief in the future value of the stock is opposite that of the seller's. This disparity is illustrated even more clearly with futures trading.

Of real interest is the academic community's belief that the markets are efficient, which assumes that traders have rational reasons for their behavior, knowing what they are doing and having a good reason for doing it. Academicians also believe that the markets are basically random, which seems to be a complete contradiction to a market that is supposed to be efficient. In fact, however, the market's behavior is mostly irrational, if you define rational as any action that is the result of a specific methodology or is planned in advance and definitely not random because irrational behavior is very predictable. If you want to learn to predict price movement, you don't need to pay attention to reasons. What you need to do is determine how the majority of traders perceive the external conditions in relationship to either their fear of scarcity, or their fear of missing out, or both.

CHAPTER 8

The Three Stages to Becoming a Successful Trader

Before we cover the three stages to becoming a successful trader, it would be a good idea to review some of the material already covered. In the market environment you have to make the rules to the game and then have the discipline to abide by these rules, even though the market moves in ways that will constantly tempt you into believing you don't need to follow your rules *this* time. This movement allows you to indulge in any illusion or distortion that suits you in any given moment. Certainly you wouldn't choose to feel pain (confronting your illusions about the market) if there is any reasonable information that would support the possibility of your expectation being fulfilled.

In an unlimited environment, if you can't confront the reality of a loss, then the possibility exists for you to lose everything, in each and every trade. If you believe trading is like gambling, it isn't. In any gambling game you have to actively participate to lose and do nothing to stop losing. In the market environment, you have to actively participate to get into a trade and actively participate to end your losses. If you do nothing, the potential exists to lose everything you own.

When you participate in gambling games, you know exactly what your risk is *and* the event always ends. With the markets you don't ultimately know what your risk is, even if you are disciplined enough to use stops, because the market could gap through your stops. Also because the event never ends and is in constant motion, there is always the possibility of getting back what you are losing in any trade. You won't need to actively participate to get back what you are losing; you just have to stay in your trade and let the market give it to you. As a result, there is the constant temptation not to cut your losses which is very difficult to resist. Why choose pain over the possibility of being made whole, when all you need do is ignore the risk.

YOU CREATE YOUR EXPERIENCE
OF THE MARKET

Each equilibrium (the current price) presents every trader with an opportunity to either buy low or sell high relative to the next change. Except for the time it takes to execute a trade, it is basically the same market for all of us. You are either able to perceive any given equilibrium as opportunity to execute a trade, or you can agonize over what you believe is a missed opportunity from the last price change, or you can refrain from taking the trade at the current price—even though you perceive it as an opportunity—because you fear the market might make you wrong. The market does not create the ways in which you perceive it; it merely reflects what is going on inside of you in any given moment.

Whether you perceived the current market condition as an opportunity and didn't act on your perception, or didn't realize it was an opportunity until after the move occurred is, again, a direct reflection of your unique psychological makeup. You attach the meaning to any particular move.

From an objective perspective the next tick up can be described as the price just moved one tick up from the previous price. That is a reality about that one-tick price change we all share. However, to one trader that one up tick could be the final defeat in a short position he had been carrying. To another trader, it could mean a perfect selling opportunity because the market just can't go higher.

To a third trader it could mean a buying opportunity because the market broke out of a resistance area, based on the way he defines resistance.

The market neither chooses nor has any way of choosing the meaning you attach to any particular price change or market condition. For example, you could perceive an opportunity to sell high and act on that perception by entering the market with a short position. From the point you entered, let's say the market went in your favor and then violently reversed itself. In doing so, it very quickly went through your entry point and kept on going up with only a few rest periods and minor little retracements.

Each rest or retracement could have been an opportunity to get out of your short position and reverse yourself. What would stop you? The answer is inside of you. If you breathed a sigh of relief each time the market paused or retraced a bit, choosing to believe it was finally all over, then I ask you, What is all over? Is it possibly the fact that you won't have to confront yourself and say I'm wrong. That again is inside of you. You choose (based on the makeup of your mental environment) to believe the pauses were stopping points, relief from confrontation, instead of a possibility to take advantage of an opportunity to eliminate your risk and a high probability to accumulate a profit by reversing yourself.

The way the market seemed to you was actually the way you created it in your own mind. Out of all the available choices and alternate ways of considering the possibilities, you choose one particular way. Your own mental framework (controlling what and the ways in which you perceive information) locked you into that losing trade. The unique way you define a loss (your beliefs about it) and what it means to you is a component part of your psychological makeup. Your beliefs will interact with your perception of environmental information to form the particular way you pick and choose whatever information you happen to focus your attention on. The market has nothing to do with this process, even though that is where the information is coming from.

In the trading environment the outcome of your decisions is immediate, and you are powerless to change anything except your mind. The power you have to create more fulfilling outcomes from your trading resides in your degree of mental flexibility. You have to learn how to flow with the markets; you are either in harmony with them or you are not. The less acceptance you have for different types of market behavior, the more the market seems to turn on you like Dr. Jekyll and Mr. Hyde. In one moment it is satisfying all your needs; in the next it is like a greedy monster taking everything away. This Dr. Jekyll/Mr. Hyde characteristic of the markets only represents your own mental inflexibility to flow with the changes and your lack of understanding—that you give yourself to the best of your ability what you end up with, out of what is available. And by the same token, what you lost, you gave away.

You can't change what the market is doing. You can only change yourself in a way that allows you to perceive what it may do next with increased clarity and objectivity. As a trader you want to know what is going to happen next, yet, how can you begin to know what could happen next, if you refuse to open yourself up mentally in ways that allow you to perceive the most likely possibilities? It is a complete contradiction in thought to want to know what is going to happen next in an event over which you have no control and at the same time to maintain a rigid mental structure that allows for only a very limited number of possibilities.

This contradiction in thought is the result of not understanding the nature of beliefs and how they limit a person's perception of environmental information. When you put on the trade, you had to have some belief about the future. What you need to do is learn how to release yourself from the demand your expectations be fulfilled exactly the way you expect them to be. Releasing yourself from the demand will allow you to shift your perspective to perceive whatever opportunities exist in the market now, as if you didn't have a trade on at all.

All of us are in a position of having to pick and choose environmental information because we can't be aware of everything at once. If you pick and choose market information on the basis of having to justify your beliefs, you are putting yourself at an extreme disadvantage. You will be excluding from your awareness information that may be more indicative of the consistency of the market and its potential to move in any given direction. And it will be extremely difficult to learn how to develop a perspective for the "big picture," by expanding your time frame perspective.

So even though you can't actually control the market's movement, you can learn how to control your perception of the market's movement in a way that allows you the maximum objectivity. Learning to perceive objectively will increase your ability to let the market tell you when to get in and when to get out. You can learn how to trade where you won't be using information to justify your beliefs but rather to perceive the most likely possibilities in any given moment. As you build a solid foundation of insight and understanding into the workings of your mental environment (which I will present in Chapters 9 through 14), you will learn how to change yourself in ways that will allow you to perceive the markets from an objective perspective and eventually trade intuitively.

What I will be offering you in the remainder of the book is a step-by-step process of how to adapt yourself to function more effectively in the trading environment. Essentially it is a process that will enable you to identify and manipulate your beliefs to be more consistent with your goals.

There are two dominant themes that form the foundation for this approach. The first we have already briefly covered, that you create the market that you experience in your own mind based on your beliefs, perceptions, intents, and rules. And, second, your trading results will be a function of the degree of skills you develop in three primary areas: perception, or your ability to perceive opportunity; execution, or your ability to execute a trade; and accumulation, or your ability to allow your account balance to grow over a period of time or series of trades.

PERCEIVING OPPORTUNITY

Your perception of opportunity is a function of the depth of insight into the market's behavior. The depth of your insight into the market's behavior is equivalent to the number of distinctions you can make and the quality of these distinctions. Perception of opportunity is synonymous with your expectation of what the market will do next. To be effective, you will need to learn how to make kinds of distinctions that will provide you with an indication of a high-probability opportunity from an objective perspective, what I call making an uncommitted assessment of the probabilities.

To be able to make some kind of quality distinctions that will eventually develop into a "vision" of the broader perspective, you will need to learn how to expand your time frame perspective of market activity. There are several components to this process, but the two most important are (1) instituting a completely disciplined trading approach and (2) learning how to release yourself from the negative emotional energy stored in the memories of any past trading experiences.

The disciplined approach will naturally help you develop the degree of self-trust essential to function effectively in an environment that does not provide any external constraints to limit or control your behavior, as society does. Without the discipline, you will be at the mercy of your own unrestrained impulses and basically out of control. Consequently, without the self-trust that develops from the self-discipline, you will fear the unpredictability of your own behavior. At the same time, you will likely project this fear into the markets as being erratic and seemingly unpredictable, when it is your own behavior you fear the most.

It would be ludicrous to think that you could understand the market's behavior to any degree greater than you understand your own behavior first. To grasp the fundamental nature of your own behavior, you will need to understand thoroughly all the effects fear has on your perception of environmental information.

At the most fundamental level, fear will limit your awareness of market information that could clearly indicate those possibilities that are in your favor and those that are not. How could any deep level of insight into the market's behavior ever develop if you are constantly worried about what the market may do to you and cannot stay focused on the consistency and structure of the market itself. The market can't do anything to you if you trust yourself to act appropriately under any market condition. Learning this is the key to gaining the level of confidence every trader needs to be successful.

In the larger perspective, fear will reduce the likelihood of you ever developing to the point of making the kinds of distinctions in market behavior where you acquire a "vision" of the big picture. When you understand how fear operates in your trading and have conquered it, you will be able to see how fear operates in the market as a whole and then be able to anticipate the group's reaction to certain kinds of information.

If you did not start your trading career with the proper mental perspective or with a disciplined approach, then it is likely you have suffered some degree of psychological damage. I define *psychological damage* as any mental condition that has the potential of generating fear. The negative energy stored in these experiences (that create and support a belief about the threatening nature of the environment) will generate fear to the same extent as the degree of energy stored in the memory.

By learning to release yourself from the pain, you will be reducing the fear and automatically opening yourself up to new awarenesses about the nature of the markets. You will be opening yourself up because fear will not be causing you to narrow your focus of attention. Instead of being focused on pain avoidance, you can be focused on what the markets are telling you. Learning how to release yourself from fear will also free you up to think of creative ways in which you can respond to the new relationships you are perceiving in the market's behavior. As a result, you will be increasing your confidence in your ability to respond appropriately to any given market situation.

EXECUTING YOUR TRADES

Your ability to execute your trades is a function of the amount of fear you generate or the lack of it. Fear is always the result of your beliefs about the threatening nature of the environment. What could be threatening about the market? Nothing, if you had the confidence and completely trusted yourself to act appropriately under any given set of market conditions. Essentially, what you fear is not the markets but rather your inability to do what you need to do, when you need to do it, without hesitation.

In your relationship with the markets you had to learn what to fear. What you learned to fear was a result of whatever you did that caused pain. Your pain was the result of your not knowing what to do next that resulted in an outcome you neither expected nor intended. In the market environment you are free to act or not to act; the markets cannot do anything to you that you don't allow, even if it is out of ignorance or a complete sense of powerlessness.

The effects of fear on one's behavior are obvious, limiting one to the point of complete immobility. If you can't execute your trades properly, even when you perceive the most perfect opportunity, it is because you have not released yourself from the pain contained in the memories of past trading experiences and because you still don't trust yourself to act appropriately in any given set of conditions. If you did, there would be no fear or immobility.

ACCUMULATING PROFITS

Your ability to accumulate profits either in a single trade or cumulatively with several trades over a period of time is a function of your degree of self-valuation. This sense of self-valuation is, in fact, the most important psychological component of success and will override all others in determining your results.

Your degree of self-valuation will regulate how much money you will give yourself (the market doesn't give you the money, you give it to yourself based on your ability to perceive opportunity and execute a trade) out of the maximum potential available or perceivable at any given moment or time frame perspective. Regardless of the depth of understanding you have of market behavior or what you consciously intend, you will only "give" yourself the amount of money that corresponds to your level of self-valuation.

This concept can be explained with a simple illustration. If you perceive an opportunity, based on your definition or what market conditions constitute an opportunity, and do not follow through by executing a trade, what stopped you? In my mind, there can be only two possible reasons. You were either immobilized by the fear of failure or you are struggling with a belief (value) system that says you don't deserve the money. Otherwise, you would have acted on your perception.

SELF-ACCEPTANCE

The second theme that provides a foundation for the belief system I am offering is that personal transformation, growth, and learning new skills are a function of self-acceptance. Your intent of learning a new skill or way of expressing yourself is in essence an attempt to create a new dimension of yourself. It is a goal you have projected out into the future that you will then attempt to fulfill by growing into it.

The market will quite naturally make you face what is inside of you on a moment-to-moment basis. What is inside of you could be confidence or fear, a perception of opportunity or loss, restraint or uncontrollable greed, objectivity or illusion. The market just reflects these mental conditions, it does not create them.

Therefore, to grow into a new expression of yourself (fulfill your goal of being a more successful trader), you will need to learn how to accept the existence of any of these negative mental conditions and the psychological components that create them. Cultivating a belief in accepting whatever you find inside of yourself will give you the base you need to work from to change these conditions.

To illustrate this concept of self-acceptance, I will relate to you an example of a floor trader who came to me for assistance because he wanted to change his trading style. When he first went down to the floor he got caught up in scalping because it seemed like the easiest way to make money. However, he soon found that trying to scalp for one or two ticks in the bond pit was just too physically exhausting because he had to compete with so many traders. So he decided that he needed to learn how to hang on to his trades for more than one or two ticks.

The first thing we did was to preplan his trades. We used some fairly simple techniques to identify intraday support and resistance points within a 7- to 10-tick range. The plan was for him to stand in the pit and wait for the price to hit his target (buy support or sell resistance), execute the trade, wait for the market to hit his objective, and then exit the trade. If the market traded through his entry point in the opposite direction by more than two or three ticks, he was supposed to execute the loss without hesitation. Based on our assessment of the reliability of the support and resistance numbers, we believed he didn't need to risk more than two or three ticks to know if the trade was going to work or not.

The first day that he tried to execute his plan, he did very well waiting for the market to hit his entry point. However, when it came time to execute the trade, he couldn't do it. He was supposed to buy at a support level, and he didn't do it because he thought it was going to keep on going lower. When the market didn't keep on going lower and bounced two and three ticks higher than what was his original entry point, he went ahead and bought one contract. From there he was supposed to wait until the market rotated back up to test the resistance which was 10 ticks higher than his originally intended entry point, but now it was only seven ticks away.

Instead of waiting for the market to rotate to his objective, he got out of the trade as soon as he had a two-tick profit. A short time later when the market rotated up to the resistance area, he did the same thing that he did in the first trade. He didn't get in at his price because he thought the market was going to keep on going; it didn't, and he sold three ticks lower than he originally intended and then got out for a one-tick profit, not waiting for a full rotation.

When we talked about what he did later on that day, he was extremely displeased with himself. He made himself accountable, but he did not do what he was supposed to. He didn't get in at the price he intended or out where he intended, "leaving several ticks on the table," so to speak. This is a very wealthy man who only had to risk two or three ticks at the most to find out if the trade was going to work and couldn't do it. By the same token, he was so desperate for a win that he couldn't wait for his profit objective, stating that he couldn't hang on because he has been burned too many times.

Obviously his backlog of negative experiences had nothing to do with the market's behavior or the probability of any particular strategy working or not. What was even more important, however, was his lack of acceptance for his current level of skill development. His intense anger over his performance clearly indicated that he could not accept where he was at or the results it produced. That first day was not a positive experience for him, even though he had his first winning day in a long time. His lack of self-acceptance certainly won't help him hang on to winning trades in the future; in fact, he will be digging himself into a deeper hole that he will eventually have to work his way out of if he wants to achieve the success he desires.

As time went by, he became increasingly more confident with his ability to define an opportunity with a high probability of success. Almost every trade he put on would immediately go in his favor, so he would rarely find himself in a losing trade. But each day was also becoming ever more exasperating because he was still only holding on for a one- or two-tick profit and leaving several ticks on the table as the market rotated to test the next level of support or resistance.

What was even more difficult for him to deal with was that many times he had bought the low or sold the high of the day. Of course, he didn't know at the time it was going to be the high or low of the day, but looking back, he just couldn't deal with the fact that he only got one or two ticks out of it.

I knew the pressure was building inside of him because each day he had more excuses related to the market for why he wasn't doing what he was supposed to and had less and less tolerance to listen to anything I had to say about the situation. All these excuses were just an indication that he would not accept who he was in relationship to who he desperately wanted to believe that he already was. He was obviously indulging himself in illusion. To be the person he wanted to believe he already was would require that he learn how to be patient, acknowledge who he now was so he could concentrate on what he needs to learn and forgive himself for what he believed to be his past mistakes and inadequacies.

However, this would be very difficult because being impatient with other people had always got him what he wanted as long as he was dealing with people who perceived themselves as weaker than he. So why should he have to learn how to be patient now? Besides if he was patient with himself, it would make it difficult to justify his impatient, intolerant stance toward others who didn't "learn" fast enough or made "mistakes."

I didn't hear from him for a while and I just assumed that he wasn't doing anything different. Then one day after the close he called to tell me that he was going to start trading a 20-contract position. Otherwise nothing else about what he was doing had changed, except that he had several winning days in a row consisting of one- and two-tick winners.

I knew he was setting himself up for a big losing day, although I didn't indicate this to him in our conversation. In his mental system he was reasoning that by trading a larger contract size he would make enough money to prove to himself and everyone else that he had finally arrived, that he was a successful trader and that he was not a person subject to deep-rooted fears. Not being one to stand in the way of "progress," all I said was that I didn't think it was very prudent for him to be trading a 20-contract position, since he hadn't developed the psychological or mechanical skills to handle a position of that size. He grunted and hung up the phone.

The next day he lost almost $3,000.00 trading 20-contract positions. He gave back to the markets all his profits, plus more, from all his successful efforts over the last two and a half weeks of trading. At that point he was ready to listen to a plan on how he could learn how to be more accepting of himself and how to hang on to his winning trades.

The following is another example of a trader who has learned self-acceptance. This trader works for a local brokerage firm, manages hedge positions for financial institutions, and also trades for his own account. I started working with him on a fairly regular basis about three years before the experience I am about to relate.

He called me one day to tell me how proud he was of reversing his position on his last trade of the day. He said he cut his losses without hesitation and reversed his position from being short to going long. He was delighted that he felt no conflict, resistance, or mental anguish. He recognized what needed to be done and he did it. However, shortly after he did his reversal, one of the floor traders, who worked for the same firm filling customer orders, called him from the floor with some friendly advice that he should get out of his long position.

Now, my client had resolved long ago that he would not place any significance on another trader's perception of the market. He had excellent knowledge of the markets and believed he could trust his ability completely to define opportunity and make assessments of the potential for the market to move. At least he thought he believed he trusted himself. After he got the phone call, he knowingly allowed himself to be influenced by what this floor trader had to say and exited his position. Within 10 minutes of doing so the market (bond) rallied 15 ticks, just about what my client originally thought it had the potential to do when he put the position on.

He left 15 ticks on the table because he let another trader influence his perception of the market. However, he did not view this experience as a missed opportunity. He viewed it as an example of how he hadn't, as of yet, completely released himself from other people's opinions of the market. He didn't miss an opportunity because given the environmental conditions he was working under (someone calling him was an environmental condition he had no control over other than not to place any significance on the information); he simply was not psychologically prepared to take advantage of the opportunity. If he had been psychologically prepared, he would have stayed with his original plan, realizing that someone else's perception of the market isn't going to be any more objective than his. Furthermore, considering the skills he had already developed, their objectivity would usually be a lot less.

As you cultivate a stronger belief in self-acceptance, you will then realize how the market reflects back to you your level of skill development along with the information that will indicate what you need to work on to become ever more successful. Each moment will then become a perfect indication of your skills and your degree of self-valuation, giving you a solid base from which to improve and learn.

You will eventually understand at a very practical level how you are always doing the best you can because your outcomes will be the result of your depth of insight into the nature of the market environment and your ability to act on whatever you perceive.

There won't be any reason not to accept these results as you increase your understanding of how to adapt yourself to suit any particular set of environmental conditions and realize the power inherent within this understanding. If you were to deny this perfection of the moment (a lack of self-acceptance), you would, in effect, be denying yourself the kind of information you need to grow into the skills you are attempting to learn. You can't grow or expand if you are denying the existence of environmental information that would clearly indicate your level of development. Nor can you acquire effective skills when you try to build from a base of illusion about the nature of the environment and yourself. If you won't acknowledge your true starting point, you cannot take the next most appropriate step in the development of any skill you intend to learn.

The most essential component in the process of transformation is learning how to recognize and then clear out beliefs that argue for the status quo, beliefs that defend against the intrusion of environmental information you refuse to consider, and learning how to read the environment in a way that will clearly point to the most appropriate path to fulfilling yourself.

PART III

Building a Framework for Understanding Ourselves

At the start of this book, I said it would be a step-by-step guide in the process of adapting yourself to the trading environment. The first step in this process of adaptation is recognizing the need to adapt. If you can't manipulate or force the markets to change in a way that suits your needs, then you will need to learn how to change yourself to suit the conditions. The market places no limits or constraints on the ways in which you choose to express yourself, in that respect; unlike in the cultural environment, you have all the power. The primary purpose of Part II, The Nature of the Trading Environment from a Psychological Perspective, was to point out some of the vast differences between the trading environment and the social environment we were taught to function in and to demonstrate clearly a need for a new perspective.

The next two steps in this process are to learn how to (1) identify exactly what changes you need to make to function successfully in the trading environment and (2) how to effect any mental changes that are necessary. Manipulating the physical environment is as easy as moving a chair from one place to another because that's where you want or need to sit. However, to consciously change yourself to function more effectively in a market environment that will not respond to your attempts to manipulate it will require a thorough understanding of the nature and functioning of your mental environment.

The types of changes you will need to make will fall into two broad categories. First, you will need to learn some sophisticated mental skills to adapt yourself more readily to the constant changes with which the market confronts you—which will require neutralizing some commonly held cultural beliefs about success. (These are the beliefs that have the potential to distort market information.) Second, you will likely need to undo any psychological injury you may have sustained from your previous trading activity. Any psychological injury diminishes your capacity to execute your trades properly.

There are obviously a multitude of substeps to learn how to identify what you need to learn, what you need to change, and how to make those changes. The six chapters in this part are organized to take you through this process of adaptation by providing you with the insight you will need to understand what you have to do and why.

The first thing you will need is a structural framework to make the things that go on in your mental environment more tangible and concrete. To give you this framework, I will describe, define, and organize the component parts of the mental environment into a manageable context to where you can (1) understand your behavior, (2) learn the various techniques for manipulating your mental environment at your conscious direction to be more consistent with the environmental conditions and your goals, and (3) learn how to monitor your relationship with the exterior environment.

It is essential that you learn how to monitor your relationship between the interior and exterior environment because our goals, intents, expectations, needs, and wants are all component parts of our mental environment that we project out into the physical environment for fulfillment in some future moment. In other words, they are all components of the mental environment that either happen or don't happen in the outside physical world. You need to be able to recognize immediately (especially as a trader) when you have the potential to distort the outside information to be consistent with the inner components. These distortions will inevitably result in pain and psychological injury.

What I intend to demonstrate in the following chapters is even though you cannot turn your eyes inward to actually see these mental component parts of the mental environment, it doesn't make them any less real. Besides, it isn't necessary to turn our eyes inward because we can just as easily learn to define what is inside of our mental environment by what we see and experience in the outside physical environment. By making the connection between what we believe and what we experience, it will be a lot easier to change what we experience by learning how to manipulate our beliefs.

We will examine the nature of beliefs and how they act as environmental information management systems. I will demonstrate how our individual beliefs about the nature of the market, and our expectations of what it will do next, manage and control the type and quality of information we perceive about it. By breaking down the dynamics of perception, you will be able to identify the various ways in which all of us place mental limitations on the market's behavior and how these limitations cause us to distort market information.

We will thoroughly explore the nature of fear and how it compels all of us to act without a perception of choice. The predominate underlying force behind most traders' actions causing prices to move is fear—the fear of missing out (competing for the supply) and the fear of loss. If you really want to understand the market's behavior to anticipate what it will do next, then you will first have to learn about and understand the underlying forces beneath your own behavior and how you process and manage information.

When you understand how any number of typical market-related fears operate in your life and learn to release yourself from them, you will, in effect, be separating yourself from the "crowd." When you separate yourself from the "crowd" and expand what you know about the forces affecting your behavior to encompass the group, it will be much easier to anticipate what the group will do because they will merely represent a larger (collective) version of the way you used to be. In other words, you will know how other traders will behave before they do because you will be able to observe them from a detached perspective—due to your having evolved beyond the choiceless state of operating out of fear.

As you gain in your understanding of how beliefs interact with environmental information to control your perception and form your experience, along with learning how to distinguish between wishful thinking and what the market is indicating about itself, you will eventually be able to learn how to control your perception of the market activity in a way that allows you the greatest amount of mental flexibility, where you will be able to shift your perspective to flow with the markets and execute your trades without hesitation. If you can't change or control what the market is doing, then the only option you have left is to control yourself in a way that allows you to perceive what the market may do next with increased clarity and objectivity, requiring a thorough working knowledge of the nature of your inner environment in relationship to the outer physical environment.

CHAPTER 9

Understanding the Nature of the Mental Environment

Understanding yourself and learning how to function inside your mental environment is not as difficult as you may think it is. It does, however, require that you gain a thorough understanding of the general characteristics of the mental environment, its component parts, and how they work, which is exactly what this part of the book is designed to give you.

The only reason why any of this would seem so difficult is because we aren't taught how to do it when we are young. In fact, we are usually taught exactly the opposite—that the mental environment is a mysterious place that can't be understood. As a result, we end up defining mental components in a haphazard fashion without ever really understanding the relationship between the components, or the relationship these components have with the outside physical environment in the ways that determine how we experience our lives. So, if you are going to consciously transform or adapt yourself to function more effectively as a trader, you will need a very fundamental and practical understanding of the nature of these mental components and how they operate. As will be explained in a moment, there are vast differences in the characteristics of the mental environment (inner) and physical environment (outer) in which our bodies occupy space. Understanding these differences is a key ingredient in the process of changing yourself.

As a simple example, the book you are reading exists on the outside of you, whereas the label of book (i.e., your mind's perception of the book) or any other thoughts or sensations you would experience as a result of that label and the meaning you attach is all occurring on the inside of you. Anything that goes on or that happens on the inside of you would constitute your mental environment; all your experiences and memories of those experiences, all your beliefs, all the emotional energy attached to those beliefs, all your feelings, needs, wants, expectations, and goals, and all your thoughts, regardless of whether or not you have expressed these thoughts into the environment, make up your mental landscape.

However, before we explore the differences between the inner and outer environments, I want to point out one characteristic common to the two. They are both constructed of many independently functioning parts ("regions" would be a better word to describe the inner environment) that cooperate to make up the whole. Most people are very familiar with their body parts, even the ones enclosed within the body cavity. These parts are made up of cells that have distinct functions. They operate independently and cooperate with the other body parts. The sum total of these cooperating parts is our body. A simple illustration would be that eyes are not ears or lungs, they are distinct parts having unique functions within the whole.

By the same token, the mental environment is composed of a number of cooperative but independently functioning regions that make-up the whole of who we are. For example, a belief is not a dream, nor is a thought an emotion. Beliefs, dreams, thoughts, and emotions are all separate parts of the mental environment that interact in the same manner (at least conceptually) that your hands will interact with your eyes or your finger with your nose or your lungs with your heart. I am pointing this out because most people do not think of their mental environments in such specific ways with highly refined distinctions among the various regions and the ways the components within those regions function.

The following list provides some of the categories into which I have divided the mental environment and the components associated with each category that will be explained in the next five chapters.

Positively Charged Emotions: Love, happiness, joy, confidence, peace, acceptance

Negatively Charged Emotions: Fear, anger, hatred, jealousy, disappointment, confusion, impatience, stress, anxiety, betrayal

Illusions: Denials, rationalizations, intellectualizations, distortions

Beliefs

Intents: Goals, aspirations

Expectations: Wants, desires, demands

Needs

Dreams: Sleeping dreams, daydreams

Thoughts

Attractions

Memories

Creativity

Intuition

This is not intended to represent a complete list of components and categories of the mental environment. However, it is comprehensive enough to serve the objectives of this book, which is to give you enough of a working knowledge of how they operate and interact to effect any changes you determine are necessary to trade successfully.

WHAT EXACTLY IS THE MENTAL (INNER) ENVIRONMENT?

I am defining the mental environment as a place where all the sensory information from the physical environment (sensory information being the way in which the physical environment acts as a force on our eyes, ears, nose, taste, and touch) gets sorted, categorized, labeled, organized, associated with, and stored. Beliefs are formed and meanings get attached. The mental environment is where our experiences of the outside world form into a complex belief structure about the nature of the physical environment and our relationship with it.

There are two things that I want you to note about this definition. First, it is limited, because it doesn't take into account mental activities that generate from within, exclusive of outside sensory information. This is something I will expand on later. Second, I am not including the brain as part of the mental environment, even though the activity of the mental environment takes place inside of the brain. (Why I am not including it will become clear in a moment.)

One of the first characteristics you may notice about the mental components listed is that they are all intangible. You can't see, hear, touch, taste, or smell them, at least not as they exist in the mental environment. For example, no surgeon operating on living brain tissue has ever encountered his patient's beliefs, thoughts, dreams, or memories, even though he knew they were in there somewhere. Biochemists have discovered DNA (deoxyribonucleic acid) while working at the molecular level of tissue make-up and as of yet have not encountered one of the mental components listed earlier. Yet we know they exist because we can experience the results of someone's beliefs or thoughts as they are expressed outwardly in the physical environment through their behavior.

Now, for those of you who are asking yourself how do these mental components exist if they aren't tangible and no one has ever directly experienced them? The answer is, they exist as a form of energy (and energy doesn't have mass). For example, light will pass through physical objects or reflect off them, but light will not displace anything, and electricity will pass through objects, not displace them. Entities made up of atoms and molecules will displace one another as they move into each other's space.

For a long time the scientific community believed that the atom was the smallest, most fundamental building block of existence, only to discover later that within an atom is energy. What scientists haven't figured out yet is how does something that exists without mass (the energy within the atom) become something that does have mass—the atom. In other words, how does energy go from being nonphysical to physical. Albert Einstein was once asked to give his definition of matter and he said "Matter is merely energy in a form that we can perceive by our senses." Even at the atomic level the book you are now reading and the chair you are sitting on to read it appear to your senses as if they are solid. However, that is not the case at all. Our senses cannot perceive things as they exist at the atomic level where everything is spinning and there is space between the atoms. However, the point I am making is that all matter exists as energy at the very deepest level of existence (within the atom), but not all energy exists as matter, as with light and electricity.

In very general terms, mental energy, as it exists in its various, intangible forms as beliefs, feelings, emotions, and so on has the potential to act as a force on our behavior and consequently as a force on the outside physical environment corresponding to the way in which this energy is expressed. For example, mental energy in the form of a belief or memory of an experience can motivate a person to walk across a room to change the channel on his television set because he believes a program on another channel is more worthwhile or pleasurable, bid the price of a stock higher than the last price because he believes it serves his best interests, or motivate masses of people to go to war to defend or promote whatever they believe needs to be defended or promoted. These actions and their effects on the environment are the result of this mental energy expressed outwardly.

WHAT IS EXPERIENCE?

We experience the world with our five physical senses. This is common knowledge. But, when you get down to the very basics, what actually happens to our experiences of the environment as they go from the outer (physical) to the inner (mental) environment? What we see, hear, touch, taste, and smell at a physical level is transformed into electrical impulses of *energy* and is sent to the brain via the nervous system. That is, at the most basic level, tangible experience of the outside world is transformed into intangible electrical energy, meaning that the tangible medium where we experience our lives (the physical environment) does not have the same characteristics and properties of the medium that represents and stores these experiences on the inside of us (the mental environment). We will examine these differences on a more practical level in a moment.

If, at first, it seems preposterous to think that our experiences (environmental information) are transformed into electrical energy, then consider that we have been using an analogous form of technology mechanically for years in the form of telephones and computers. Computers store information, sounds, and images in a number of different energy media. Telephones transport sounds and images in the form of electricity, light, or microwaves. As commonplace as all this is, there is still something fascinating about a living process that transforms sensory information (tangible experience) into electricity and stores it that way. Everything that we have learned (as individuals) about the nature of our existence is stored in our mental environment at an intangible level, in a nonphysical reality (energy is real, yet it is nonphysical because it doesn't consist of atoms and molecules, thus it can be said that energy exists in a nonphysical reality).

Earlier, I did not include the brain as part of the mental environment because it exists at the tangible level of atoms and molecules (physical reality), whereas the mental environment (energy in the form of beliefs, memories, emotions, and so on, about the nature of physical environment resulting from our experiences) does not exist at this tangible level. To help you understand this distinction between the brain and the mental environment, consider that the brain exclusive of the mental environment is no different from a computer that is not plugged into some electrical power source. In this analogy, the mental environment would correspond to the electrical energy that makes the computer run as well as store and carry the various forms of information the computer is designed to handle and the computer hardware (physical, mechanical, atoms, and molecules) would correspond to the brain.

This is the reason why I stated in the beginning of the chapter that there are vast differences between the mental and physical environments. All the mental components I listed exist at the intangible level of energy and, more important, function with the same properties and characteristics of energy. To understand the nature of the mental environment, you need to understand the characteristics of energy. Thus, what I intend to do next is examine the properties and characteristics of typical energy forms like light and electricity and then compare them to the characteristics of the mental environment to establish a correspondence between the two.

Finally, in the next five chapters I will tie all this material together to give you some very practical techniques to improve your ability to trade effectively.

HOW DOES THE MENTAL ENVIRONMENT CORRESPOND TO THE CHARACTERISTICS AND PROPERTIES OF ENERGY?

Energy Is Nondimensional

As we already know, energy doesn't take up space in the physical environment because it doesn't displace anything that does take up space. This "no space" characteristic of energy gives it a nondimensional quality. In other words, anything that doesn't take up space also won't have any tangible dimensions of height, length, width, or circumference, at least not in the ways in which we would normally think of these properties. This nondimensional quality is probably the hardest concept to grasp about the nature of energy, because even though energy is nondimensional, it can take some form that is visible to our eyes. And anything that is visible should have dimensions that we can measure. It may seem like an obvious contradiction to say that energy can take a visible form and yet still not have dimension, but it is not.

The best example to illustrate this is with holograms or holographic photography. With a holographic process you can create a three-dimensional image in light projected into space that can be seen with the eyes, and it will appear to have length, width, and circumference. You could even measure the length or width of the image; however, your hands would pass right through the image if you tried, because there really isn't anything there, at least not in a physical sense. Images in light have no physical substance, so from a physical perspective, they also don't have any dimension. (Relative to physical objects, energy doesn't have dimension.)

Memories or mental images (anything that we can see with our inner eye, like visualizations, daydreams, or night dreams) could operate very much like a hologram of laser light—an image of light that has no physical substance—where space as it relates to distance or dimension is not a consideration. The total area available inside of our skulls is quite small, especially in relationship to what will fit from a mental perspective. We can create mental images of any size or proportion, with none of the dimensional limitations that exist in the physical environment because these images, as an energy form, have no physical substance and thus exist in a state of form without dimension, taking up "no space."

You can easily demonstrate this concept with a simple mental exercise. Close your eyes and picture the last place where you went on a vacation. Where did you stay? What side trips did you take? When you imagined where you went, did you get up and move from your present location in the physical environment. Did you imagine yourself getting up out of your chair to make all the preparations that would be necessary for such a trip? Did you get in your car and mentally drive each mile to your destination, as you would if you were actually going? Probably not; the image of your last vacation most likely just popped into your consciousness. It is as if you were instantaneously transported to these locations, without regard to the space or distance that you would need to travel to get there in the physical environment. There was "no space" between your present location and the image of the vacation spot you hold in your memories.

The nature of our dreams also illustrates this nondimensional characteristic. First, there is no known limit to the type of dream landscape we could find ourselves in. Dreams can be as varied and diverse, if not more so, as the physical environment and all much larger than the space available inside of our skull cavity. Furthermore, in our dreams we can instantaneously change locations without actually traveling any distance. For example, you could dream that you are in the basement of your house and then in the next instant be in your living room, without actually having walked up your basement stairs or through other rooms to get to there.

Speed

The second characteristic the mental environment shares with energy is speed. Energy travels at an incredibly high rate of speed. Light, for example, travels at a rate of 186,000 miles per second, fast enough to travel around the Earth approximately eight times in 1 second. This is so fast that to our physical senses, it appears instantaneous or simultaneous. What I mean is, it moves so fast that our physical senses cannot detect the motion. Obviously, we can see the light, but we cannot actually see it moving from any given source to some distant point. For example, when you turn on a light in a dark room, does the room become illuminated in stages as the light travels from its source to the walls? No, to our eyes the room fills with light instantaneously, seeming to be everywhere at once, in a flash. Our eyes are not constructed in a manner where we can make any distinctions in movement, so it seems as if it doesn't move at all.

This instantaneous characteristic of light relates quite well to the mental environment. As I pointed out earlier, dream travel can be and usually is instantaneous. While you're having a dream, in one instant you could be in a house and the next you could be on the other side of the world. There really isn't any travel time between these dream locations. Whatever, mental mechanism prompts the change, it creates a simultaneous transfer, probably taking as much physical (clock) time as it does for light to fill up a dark room.

However, there is another mental characteristic (actually more of a phenomenon) that best illustrates the speed at which the mental environment operates. This is something that is not experienced by very many people, but nevertheless reported by enough people in completely separate, unrelated incidents to confirm its validity. What I am referring to is the phenomenon of having one's life flash before one's consciousness in the form of a continuous mental image, from birth to the present. Something like this usually only happens in extreme life-threatening situations where the person believes that he is only moments from death. In those few moments before the expected death, the sights, sounds, tastes, smells, feelings, and emotions of one's entire life are reexperienced.

Personally whenever I've read of or heard someone's recounting of such an experience, it baffled me. I didn't understand how a person's whole life could scroll before his consciousness in a matter of moments, when it took years to experience. However, after a great deal of contemplation, it occurred to me that the energy in which our experiences are stored moves at speeds that are so incredibly fast that it would make our lives seem quite short in comparison, thus making it possible for all our experiences to scroll by in moments, regardless of how long it took actually to have the experiences.

All this might be a little easier to understand if you imagine, as I did, experiences stored in a stream of light very much like what you would see when you look at a distant star. There is a very good correlation here. For example, scientists tell us that many of the closest stars to the Earth, other than our sun, are so far away, that even at the incredible speed of 186,000 miles per second, it still takes the light emanating from these stars hundreds of years to reach the Earth. This distance between the stars and Earth is so vast that it creates a steady beam of light, billions of trillions of miles long. So, when we look at any star other than our sun, what we are actually seeing is the light that left it hundreds or even thousands of years ago, thus what we are seeing is light from the star's distant past. Now, if we could travel along this beam of light back to its source, what we would be seeing is light from the star's more recent past (or future from the perspective of traveling toward the star) the closer that we got to it, until we arrived at the star's present. Light from the past, future (depending on one's perspective), and present would exist simultaneously within that beam.

Now, imagine the sights, sounds, tastes, smells, feelings, and emotions of our experiences stored in energy as a stream of memories that we can travel along very much like this beam of light, where we can use our consciousness to roam between the distant past to the more recent past up to the present moment or project these memories out into the future. If the energy in which our experiences are stored can move at speeds that are equal to or approach the speed of light, then it would offer a credible explanation as to how it is possible for one's whole life to scroll before one's consciousness in a matter of moments. To illustrate this for yourself further, imagine all your experiences stretched out like a beam of light that you could travel along at the speed of light. At that speed, at even a couple of seconds of travel time, you could get through a great deal of information. For example, if we just arbitrarily decided that it took 10,000 miles of mental energy stretched out to hold 1 year's worth of experience, then, at the speed of light, you could get through almost 19 years of memories in 1 second.

Recognition of this phenomenon helps us to grasp one of the most difficult concepts about the nature of the mental environment—that it exists outside of time, as we know it. That is, our physical senses lock us into perceiving an environment bounded by the limitations of time and three-dimensional space. We have to experience each moment in a linear sequence. We can't go backward and experience the past as it existed in the physical environment; once it passes, it's gone forever. Nor can we move ahead into the future. The past doesn't exist anymore, and the future doesn't exist yet. What does exist are these seemingly endless sequences of "now moments" in which we experience our lives. However, the mental energy our inner components consist of operates outside of our normal concept of time and space as it is experienced in the physical environment. In the mental environment there are no spatial boundaries or time constraints; we can think in any direction we please: past, present, or future. And, theoretically, there would be no limits or boundaries as to how much information could be stored.

Simply stated, time is a function of our perception of movement over distance or three-dimensional space. In other words, to perceive time, you need two key components: space that has dimensions, and movement. Both these properties obviously exist in the physical environment. It has characteristics of three-dimensional space consisting of length, height, width or thickness, and circumference. Also the physical environment is in constant motion. The sun, other stars, the planets, and their moons are all in motion. And even though we can't directly perceive it, everything physical is in motion at the atomic and molecular level. Everything is spinning around something larger from the tiniest atoms and molecules to the largest stars and solar systems, including the atoms and molecules in our own bodies.

This spinning motion of the Earth and its orbit around the sun acts as a force on the environment, changing day to night and night to day, creating the weather and the seasons as well as an endless number of other environmental cycles. All these cycles of environmental changes (including our own bodily cycles of growth, age, respiration, digestion, and so on, resulting from the movement of the atoms and molecules of our cells) act as a force on our physical senses, causing us to experience a constantly changing environment, one cycle after another, in straight linear fashion, thus giving us our perception of time that is always moving forward. If we couldn't perceive motion or some sort of movement over three-dimensional space to act as reference points to measure this movement, then we wouldn't be able to perceive the passing of time. For example, if we were conscious but somehow fixed in a state of suspended animation where we had no sensory input, no perception of movement of any kind, not even a heartbeat, it would be impossible to tell the difference between a few seconds or a few days. To measure time, you need a point to start from and a point to get to; these points can be measured off in distance or time, but you need three-dimensional space to get your points.

We think in an environment that is more like a stream where our consciousness can roam freely between the past, present, and future without regard to time or space. Furthermore, the actual sequences of moments that exist in the physical environment have no effect on the energy our memories are stored in. Sequences of time only have an effect on the mental environment relative to the impact the environment is having on our senses in energy terms. You can easily demonstrate this to yourself by trying to reconstruct from your memory the last 24 hours, moment for moment. Difficult, isn't it. Now try to do it for a week ago today. The only things we remember are the significant events, the experiences that had the most impact on our senses, the ones with the most energy connected with them. That's because experiences are not recorded in our memories as moments of time; they are stored as charges of energy. And as such they have no relationship to the passing of physical clock time.

Remember, energy doesn't exist as atoms and molecules and therefore relative to our perception of the passing of time, it is not subjected to this nonstop spinning of everything that is physical. Energy can remain static or be active. For example, someone or something could remind you of an experience that happened 20 years ago, an experience that you haven't thought of since it happened. When you tap into the energy of those memories, you will reexperience the sights, sounds, tastes, smells, and most important, the emotions of that time, as if nothing had changed. In your mind nothing has changed. The energy remained dormant for 20 years. It becomes active either when we choose to think or reflect about what is inside of us or when we are inadvertently reminded of what is inside of us.

Significantly positive (pleasurable: happy, joyful, etc.) or negative (painful: terrorizing, angry, hateful) experiences are easily recalled because of the amount or intensity of the energy involved with the event. These types of experiences will pop into our conscious recollection, at will. But, try to remember every time in your life that you brushed your teeth, took a drink of water, opened your refrigerator door, or put your shoes and socks on and it's not so easy. These events are difficult to recall because there is very little energy connected with each of these types of experiences.

Our memories are like pockets of energy that we may organize chronologically by date and time, as in the stream-of-light example. However, all the uneventful moments between the eventful moments seem to disappear without a trace or get compressed as if they never happened, even though we know that they did. We must have put on our shoes and socks a month ago today because we probably would remember walking around without them; that might be significant enough to remember.

What we read, as an example, is usually quickly forgotten because there is very little impact the environment is having on our senses. Printed words on a page have very little visual impact in relationship to activities of a more experiential nature. For example, actually participating in a biology experiment will have a much greater impact from an energy perspective than will reading about one. The energy required to remember something that we read has to be generated from within in the form of concentration.

So, the way in which we experience clock time is in relationship to what we are feeling (either physical or emotional impact) in any given moment. If, for example, you were experiencing terror, each second of clock time could easily seem like an hour or day. Each moment of a terrorizing experience seems to last forever because the environment is assaulting our senses. The impact is so painful that we can't wait for the experience to end to be out of that situation. We would therefore focus our attention on how long the event is lasting, while we were waiting for it to end, thus slowing down our sense of time.

Pleasurable experiences seem to fly by (we have no concept of time passing) because we are in a state of joy and happiness, and nothing takes us out of these moments to feel something less than the joy. We come out of that state of mind when the experience starts to diminish in its degree of happiness causing us to focus more on the unpleasantness of what we are experiencing (some degree less than joy, even if it is boredom) compared to the happiness we were feeling. When our focus shifts from joy (no concept of time passing) to "I can't wait for this to end," our sense of time slows down in proportion to the unpleasantness of the experience.

In the physical environment, experiences take place in moments of time that pass one after another, in linear fashion. What we experience in moments of time (through our physical senses) is transformed into electrical energy and stored as a memory relative to the degree of impact of the experience. Memories don't have any restrictions imposed on them by time because energy isn't physical. Time is one directional, whereas in our mental environment we are free to think about our memories at will or by just wanting to. We can experience them as a mental image, mental sounds, mental tastes, and so on. *Each of our memories makes up a part of our identity, and because they exist as an energy form, they have the potential to act as a force on our behavior.* Regardless of whether we are conscious of these specific forces or not they cause us to move through the environment in certain ways corresponding to what we have already experienced to create more experiences and more memories.

Essentially, what I am stating is that our existence straddles two very different dimensions simultaneously. We live in and perceive three-dimensional space, and, as a result, our physical senses are subject to the limitations of time, where one moment passes after another in straight linear fashion, whereas we think in a dimension where time and space as it is perceived in the physical environment doesn't exist. Now, there are some very important psychological implications within the concept that time and space don't exist in the mental environment, implications that have to do with our ability to experience happiness, fulfill our needs, and achieve our goals, which are all basically synonymous. However, before we address these implications, you will need to understand how experiences are stored in varying degrees of positively or negatively charged energy, what I call the "quality of energy" our memories are stored in.

CHAPTER 10

How Memories, Associations, and Beliefs Manage Environmental Information

From the moment we are born into this world, our existence acts as a force on the physical environment. We take up space that cannot be occupied by anyone or anything else. And, in turn, the physical environment acts as a force on our physical senses, creating a cause-and-effect relationship between ourselves and the environment. It is important for you to note now and for the rest of the book that I am defining the physical environment in the broadest sense possible, as everything outside of ourselves, including other people. Now, at the most basic level, we create experience for ourselves by the mere fact that we exist. To exist implies that our senses are alive and that we are interacting (acting as a force) with the environment, altering its makeup and consistency as we move through it. For example, our movement and behavior set off an endless series of chain reactions that alter the landscape in some way, shape, or form. And even when we aren't actively changing or manipulating the environment in some way, we are still taking up space and thus subjecting ourselves to atmospheric forces, as well as causing changes in the makeup of the atmosphere from our breathing.

MEMORIES ARE STORED AS CHARGED ENERGY

The experiences that result from this constant interaction with the environment will be transformed into electrical impulses of energy. As electrical impulses of energy, the experiences will carry an electrical charge. The charge will be either positive or negative, depending on the kind of impact the environment had on our senses. For example, a crying baby is acting as a force on the environment. More specifically, the baby is creating a sound that is acting as a force on the eardrums of everyone in his vicinity. How the environment responds to this force will create experience for the child and determine the electrical charge or quality of energy that is recorded in the baby's memory.

"Quality of energy" is the relative degree of positively or negatively charged energy in which the experience is recorded. For example, if the environment responds to the child with a soothing caress, expressing love and a sense that his needs will be taken care of, then the experience will be recorded in the child's memory with some degree of positively charged emotional energy. The degree of positiveness will depend on the intensity of the experience, that is, the degree of impact the environment had on the child's senses. Pleasant, happy, joyful, and loving experiences will result in the storage of positively charged energy. If, however, the environment responds harshly, in such a way as to have a violent impact on the child's senses, by screaming (assaulting his eardrums) or slapping him to produce physical pain, then the experience will be recorded in the child's memory with negatively charged emotional energy to the same degree as the intensity of the experience.

There are two basic components that make up the quality of energy in which our memories are stored. The first is the polarity of the charge, which could be positive, neutral, or negative. The second component is the intensity of the charge ranging from extreme positive, which would be an experience of maximum intensity creating a feeling of elation, to extreme negative, which would be an experience of unbridled terror. Quality of energy is an important concept for you to understand because it affects the type of beliefs we form about the nature of the environment, which in turn affects how we perceive information and interact with the environment.

The Characteristics of Positively Charged Energy

Positive energy is expansive. It promotes mental growth or learning by creating a sense of confidence, which in turn results in an openness to explore and discover the unknown. I am defining the unknown as anything that exists as a possibility in the physical environment that does not yet reside in some form in one's mental environment. Positive energy perpetuates our natural, childlike sense of curiosity and wonderment toward the environment that we are all born with.

By following the interests of our natural sense of curiosity, we interact with the environment to create experience and learn something previously unknown to ourselves, thus generating a sense of excitement about life, as well as increasing our ability to operate in the environment more effectively because we are continuing to learn more about the way things exist. There is a direct relationship between how much we have allowed ourselves to learn about the nature of the environment and the degree of negatively charged energy in our mental environment. I am stating it this way with the emphasis on the negative because learning will take place quite naturally if there isn't anything in the inner environment to stop it. In other words, an absence of fear (negatively charged energy) is a critical factor in determining whether or not we will make ourselves available to learn anything new and continue to grow mentally.

For example, playfully throw a child up in the air and catch him and he will beg you to do it over and over again. This is his way of interacting with the environment to perpetuate the feelings of a positively charged experience. Positive energy is expansive, compelling us to interact with the environment to create more experience for ourselves. The more we experience the more we learn about the nature of the environment. The more we learn about the nature of the environment, the better able we are to interact with it more effectively to fulfill our needs and achieve our goals. Positively charged memories give us that sense of confidence that allows to step out to try something new resulting in mental growth.

The Characteristics of Negatively Charged Energy

Now, throw the same child up in the air for the first time, as in the earlier example, but instead of catching him, accidentally drop him, and not only will he not ask you to do again, he will cower in terror at the very suggestion. The difference in his behavior, of course, is the result of the differences between the two experiences. In the first example, the experience was pleasurable, resulting in the storage of positively charged energy. In the second example, the experience was painful, resulting in the storage of negatively charged energy.

Regardless of whether we were acting as a force on the environment (behavior motivated by our sense of curiosity) and got an unexpected or unintended painful reaction, or the environment, uninitiated by ourselves (other than the fact that we exist), acted as a force on us in a way that resulted in pain, the experience will result in the formation of a negatively charged memory. Painful memories will generate fear, causing us to perceive the environment as threatening in its ability to cause more pain in some future moment. The way we will perceive it as threatening will correspond to our memories of the experiences that resulted in pain in similar circumstances or conditions (the things we fear in the environment are those things we have learned to recognize as threatening).

In contrast to the feelings of confidence and well-being that result from positively charged experiences, fear acts as a limiting or inhibiting force on both our behavior and our perception of environmental information. I am sure that everyone reading this book at some point has experienced the effects that fear can have on one's behavior. It can cause us to run from an obviously dangerous situation or completely immobilize us to the point where our body will not respond to any conscious command. Fear drastically limits our choices. It causes us to interact with the environment in ways that are limited to the structure of our memories, regardless of what the environment may be offering in the way of a new experience, or it causes us to avoid an experience completely. Interacting with the environment results in experience, and experience results in learning. If we experience the environmental present based on our individual past, or completely avoid experience altogether, we aren't learning what is being offered or available to be learned about the nature of the environment.

The net result of a painful experience is that it creates a negatively charged memory, which in turn creates and perpetuates a cycle of fear. Cycles of fear then create cycles of discontent and dissatisfaction because we avoid experience. When we avoid experience, we cut ourselves off from the joy we feel when we are learning. Just as positive cycles are expansive, negative cycles are degenerative. Our painful memories keep us from learning how to interact with the environment in effective and satisfying ways that would result in happier and more fulfilling lives because we aren't learning what we need to know to experience something different.

Fear limits both our range of behavior and our perception of environmental information. The ways in which it limits our behavior are obvious. However, there are many ways in which fear acts on our perception that aren't so obvious; in fact some of the ways can be very subtle and difficult to recognize, until one learns what to look for. As traders, it is essential that you be able to observe the market's behavior from an objective perspective. To observe objectively you will need to learn how to recognize a variety of subtle fears that will destroy your ability to be objective without really knowing it. This is a subject I will cover in much greater depth a little further on. However, before I can do so you need to understand the nature of associations and how perception creates an energy loop between the inside mental environment and the outside physical environment.

ASSOCIATIONS

Associations seem to be a natural characteristic of the way in which we think. That is, our brains are wired in such a way as to link similar forms of environmental information together automatically. We do this in basically two ways. First, there is a natural propensity to label people and objects based on some prominent characteristic and then categorize them into associative groups. After we categorize the groups by sex, hair color, skin color, profession, economic status, educational background, and so on, we then associate whatever experience or knowledge we have about the group with everyone and everything that has those same characteristics. For example, if we have a painful experience with a person who has a skin color different from that of our own, we will automatically associate everyone with that skin color with the qualities of that one experience.

The second way we associate is by linking extraneous sensory information with some event. We will automatically associate what we are smelling, tasting, hearing, or seeing along with the quality of energy of the primary experience. For example, a child getting spanked will associate all the other environmental information that his senses are inadvertently picking up with the pain he is feeling from the spanking. What he hears, smells, tastes, and sees will all be connected with the intensity of the force being applied to his body. So if there was some song playing on the radio or a distinctive odor in the air at the same time that he was experiencing pain, he will associate the song or the odor with the pain.

Now, both these environmental distinctions (a certain song and a certain smell) will be connected with negative energy in his mental environment. When the child was getting his spanking he may not have even noticed either the song or the smell because his attention was obviously focused in other directions. However, in the future whenever he hears that song or smells that particular odor, they will automatically cause him to experience the negative energy connected with the spanking. Even if it is years later, and he is enjoying himself with the last thing on his mind being the memory of that spanking, if he hears that particular song or smells that particular odor, it will carry him back to that time as if it were the present moment, changing his experience from happiness to anger, sadness, or guilt.

Of course, this same principle also works for positive experiences. A perfect example is many couples have "a song" that they associate with some intense sexual or loving experience. When they hear "their song," it will mentally put them into the feelings of the experience the song is associated with. In fact, the song can eventually come to symbolize the quality of the entire relationship where all the memories and emotions connected to those memories will run though their consciousness upon hearing the song.

Associations are an automatic function of the way in which information gets organized in our mental systems. Most of these associations are inadvertent, meaning we have positively or negatively charged energy connected to various elements of the environment, and we aren't consciously aware of it. We can see, hear, taste, or smell certain things that, in turn, cause us to feel emotions and not know why because we don't consciously remember connecting the extraneous sensory information with the primary event.

THE ENERGY LOOP BETWEEN THE
PHYSICAL AND MENTAL ENVIRONMENTS

None of us has access to "all" the environmental information that exists in any given moment. Our senses aren't constructed to allow us to pick up (see, hear, touch, taste, or smell) everything at once. If we can't be aware of it all, then we must have some mechanism by which we pick and choose what we do become aware of and give our attention and consideration to. What we learn creates an energy loop between the inner and outer environment. We can call this energy loop perception. "Perception" is recognizing—with our eyes, ears, nose, taste, and touch—in the physical environment what we have already learned about it. Mental energy works in conjunction with our physical senses to separate, categorize, and organize environmental information based on the distinctions we have learned to make. We recognize what we have learned in the environment because it is already inside of us. There has to be a mental framework to accept the information; otherwise, it gets rejected, labeled as meaningless, or not perceived at all, unless of course we are willing to construct a framework for it—being open to learn.

Distinctions

Distinctions make separations in environmental information where no previous separation existed. A child won't make a distinction between a spoon and pencil until someone teaches him the difference. Otherwise, he will instinctively put both in his mouth, until the information stored in his mental environment acts as a force on his perception to distinguish between the two. Environmental objects give off information about themselves, but the information that is perceived already exists inside of each individual, unless it is a first-time experience. The spoon and the information about what it is create an energy loop between the inside and the outside, where before the distinction was learned the spoon and the pencil would fall into the same category as something to put into the mouth. Anything we don't know, but exists in the environment as a possibility, is a distinction that we haven't learned to make yet. If we haven't learned to make the distinction, we won't perceive the various types of information the environment is giving off about itself.

For example, if I were to open up my computer, what I would perceive would be very different from that of a skilled computer repair technician. All the various parts giving off information about themselves would mean almost nothing to me because there is no meaning inside of me. All the parts my eyes would be seeing would fall into that one large category because I haven't learned to make any distinctions between the various parts, whereas the technician would perceive the parts in a very different way because he understands the functioning of the parts and the relationship that they have with one another. That understanding is the mental framework that structures the particular way in which he perceives the parts. The parts would be giving off information about themselves that I couldn't perceive because I don't have the mental structure to perceive it.

Learning how to read the markets to recognize an opportunity is another example to illustrate this energy loop between the inside and outside that we call perception. Traders act as a force on the market to move prices. Since most traders don't plan their trades or want to take responsibility for their outcomes they are highly susceptible to acting out of any number of fears. Traders who are motivated to act out of fear generally aren't aware that their fear drastically reduces the choices they perceive as available, making their behavior very predictable to an objective observer (someone not caught in the same cycles of fear). So under certain market conditions large groups of traders will all be trying to do the same thing—because of what they fear will or won't happen—upsetting the equilibrium, forcing prices to move in one direction. If you haven't yet learned to identify these conditions, you naturally won't perceive them when they exist because there has to be an energy loop between the inner and outer environments for perception to occur.

I am sure everyone has had the experience of reading unfamiliar material a second, third, or fourth time and perceiving something new with each subsequent reading. What is happening here? With each reading you are building a mental framework that enables you to recognize what was available but unperceivable to you when it was read previously. That is, all the new insight that you garner with each reading was available from the book the moment you picked it up the first time. However, you weren't able to perceive what it had to offer in the way of insights or understandings until you created an energy loop that enabled you to perceive it; otherwise, the words get read but the insight goes by completely unnoticed even though you are looking right at it.

In any given moment there is a vast difference between what each of us perceives and what is actually available in the way of possible distinctions from the environment's perspective. Take, for example, a salesperson who has learned to recognize the exact, most appropriate moment to ask for the order and close a sale. Or an auto mechanic who knows exactly what is wrong with a car by the kind of sounds that it makes. To the inexperienced salesperson or auto mechanic, these abilities will seem like magic because they will assume that they are hearing or seeing the same things as their experienced counterparts. However, that is not the case. They are not hearing or seeing the same information even though they are in the same sales interview or listening to the same car at the exact same moment. They are actually perceiving different environmental information because of the differences in the structure of their respective mental environments. The information that indicates the exact moment to ask for the order to close the sale is indistinguishable from everything else to the inexperienced salesperson. The same is true for the inexperienced auto mechanic. Consequently, neither one will perceive the existence of this information until they learn to make the appropriate distinctions. If someone wasn't there to teach them how to make these more refined distinctions that indicate the most appropriate moment to ask, they may never know about the existence of such information. By learning to make more distinctions, we increase the depth of our level of understanding of the cause-and-effect relationship between everything that exists.

How Our Perceptions Shape Our Experiences

We experience the environment through our senses. At the most fundamental level the world gets transformed into electrical impulses of energy, energy that carries information, as well as feelings and emotions ranging from extreme happiness to rage, elation to despair, love to hate, and all the degrees of feelings and emotions in between. Each first-time encounter with the environment creates a memory, distinction, or association that didn't exist previously. A first-time encounter is any experience that is completely unique, like learning the meaning of a word that we have never heard before, and there is nothing in our mental environment to relate it to. These new memories, distinctions, and associations build into a mental framework that constitute what we have learned about the nature of the outside environment.

Once we learn something, mental energy will then act as a force on our senses to recognize in the environment what we have learned about it. So there is a two-way flow of energy; first, we learn something through some unique experience; then, we perceive what we have learned in the environment. Fear is a perfect example for illustrating this concept. We feel fear when we recognize in the environment anything that we have learned can cause us pain. We will feel this fear and consequently have a fearful experience because the negatively charged energy in our memories, distinctions, and associations will act as a force on our eyes, ears, nose, and sense of touch to recognize in the environment anything that is similar to what we have already learned can cause pain.

So when we perceive something (recognizing what we have already learned) in the environment, mental energy is acting as a force on our senses, instead of the environment acting as a force on our senses. In other words, the conditions are similar or identical to what we already know, and we can therefore attach some meaning to the information. The environment isn't creating the meaning as in a first-time encounter; the meaning is already inside of us, and in essence we create the experience by the way in which we perceive it, through our memories, distinctions, and associations.

This is why a group of people can all be in the same location, be exposed to the same environmental information, and then afterward describe the event in a different way. The event was different for each individual because everyone experienced it differently. Their experience was a function of the structure of their mental environment. Each individual will make different associations with the same information and then experience the varying degrees of positive or negative energy connected with those associations. Each individual will make different distinctions with the same information, in effect placing a different meaning on it. Each meaning will be composed of varying degrees of positive or negative energy, thereby creating a different experience relative to everyone else's. Each person will experience the amount of time the event took differently, depending on whether they are perceiving the experience with predominately positively charged energy (time speeds up) or negatively charged energy (time slows down). Without taking all these mental variables into consideration, it is little wonder why people get so frustrated with one another when they can't agree on what happened. Everybody's version of what happened was unique, because the way each of us experience the outside environment is determined by how we perceive it, and how we perceive it is a function of what is already inside of us unless we are in the process learning something new.

The implications are that much of what we experience of the outside environment is shaped from the inside, not from the outside as most people would assume. In other words, our first-time experiences shape the meaning, as well as determine the quality of energy connected with that meaning, and then once the meaning exists inside of us, it shapes our experience of the outside by the way we pick and choose information and how we feel about that information.

This is a very important concept, so I will give you another example to illustrate how our perceptions shape the way we experience the environment. Let's say that I am approaching a statue of a man. At first, I look at the statue face to face, and I experience indifference; that is, what I am seeing does not evoke any particular emotion. Then, I walk around the statue, and change my viewing angle until I look at it in profile. As I look at the profile, the face reminds me of a someone (an association) whom I like very much and whom I haven't seen for years. From this new perspective the statue would take on a new meaning changing my experience from emotionally neutral to some strong feelings of nostalgia as I think about how much I miss this person.

The energy for how I experienced that statue and that particular moment in the environment was inside of me before I even looked at it. The energy that changed the feelings I was experiencing did not come from the statue or really have anything to do with that statue. My unique mental structure caused me to experience that statue the way in which I did. It took on a new meaning as I changed my perspective because of the way the energy that was already inside of me acted on my perception. If I hadn't had the positive experiences with the person the statue reminded me of, then I would have continued to experience indifference as I looked at it.

THE RELATIONSHIP BETWEEN PERCEPTIONS AND EMOTIONS

The energy that determines how we feel (love/hate, happiness/ anger, confidence/fear, etc.) in many circumstances and situations *does not* come from the environment. These feelings and emotions are already part of us, and we will automatically feel them when there is a matchup (perception) between what is outside in the now moment with what is already inside of us as a result of our past experiences. For example, imagine a father holding his five-year-old son with one hand, screaming "you stupid idiot" while spanking him with the other hand. And let's assume that this is the first time the child has heard the words stupid or idiot. Now he may not know what the words mean in an adult context, but he will most certainly connect the words with pain he is feeling through both his body as well as his ears. From that point forward these words will have a strong negative charge attached to them in his mental environment.

Now, when he encounters these words in the environment again in some future moment he will be able to recognize them because he has experienced these words—they exist as a distinction in his mental environment. As a result of the way in which he learned the meaning of these words, how will his perception of them affect his experience of them? Whenever he hears the words "stupid" or "idiot" he will feel the negatively charged energy connected to these words in his mental environment and consequently experience the physical environment in a painful way. Does the environment need to physically assault him, as in the first experience, for him to feel this pain? No. All he has to do is hear the words and he will experience pain. After his first encounter with these words, the pain doesn't have to come directly from the environment because it is already inside of him. Would it make any difference if from the environment's perspective that the words were spoken with absolutely no intent to cause him any pain or without any awareness that they could, in fact, cause him to feel pain. Again, no. He would not be able to perceive the intent of the environment as anything but wanting to cause him pain because that is exactly what he experiences when he hears those words. How could he know that other alternative meanings exist for these words or that they can also be used within a context of good-natured fun? He couldn't, because he has never experienced those words in any kind of fun context, he hasn't learned to make that distinction yet. From the perspective of his mental environment, there are no other alternative possibilities for the meaning of these words. Furthermore, he may never learn to make any alternative distinctions, because every time he hears the words "stupid" or "idiot," he will perceive them in a painful way, thereby creating an experience of pain, which will in turn reinforce the negative energy already connected to the meaning for those words. From the first experience forward into the future, he will be locked into only one version of the way he can experience those words.

In any given moment, there are a whole range of experiences available from the environment. What we experience as individuals will be a function of what we perceive, unless we are in a learning mode. In other words, what we are experiencing in any given moment is being shaped by what is already inside of us (memories, distinctions, associations, and beliefs), and what is already inside of us may not be remotely close to what the environment is offering in the way of experience. When we are in a learning mode we open ourselves up to learn new distinctions and alternative meanings to expand what we know about the nature of the environment.

Our experiences shape our meanings and then the meanings shape our experiences of the future. Let me illustrate this concept for you. I was watching a local television program in spring 1987 called "Gotcha Chicago." It was about some local celebrities who played practical jokes on other Chicago notables. In one segment of the program the TV station hired a man to stand on the sidewalk along Michigan Avenue holding a sign that read "FREE MONEY— TODAY ONLY." (For those of you who are not familiar with Chicago, Michigan Avenue is home to many of the most expensive and fashionable department stores and boutiques in the city.) The man's pockets were stuffed with cash, and he had been instructed to give money to anyone who asked for it. Considering that Michigan Avenue is one of the busiest areas of the city, how many people do you think took him up on his offer and asked for some money?

Out of all the people who walked by and read the sign, only one person stopped and said, " Great! May I have a quarter to buy a bus transfer?" Otherwise, no one would even go near him. Eventually he grew frustrated and started crying out, "Do you want any money? Please take my money. I can't give it away fast enough." Everybody just walked around him as though he didn't exist. He approached one businessman asking, "Would you like some money?" And the man responded, "Not today." The "plant" said, "How many days does this happen?" as he tried to give him a handful of cash, while continuing to say "Would you please take this?" The businessman responded with a terse "no" and walked on.

Now here is a situation where the environment was expressing itself in a way that only one person had the mental structure to perceive. For the rest of the people, there was no meaning inside of them that they could directly correlate with the actual environmental conditions. Other than the one person who asked for a quarter, nobody looked at the sign and said to themselves "Great! Somebody is giving away free money, I wonder how much he will give me."

People's responses to the conditions shouldn't be too surprising because we generally don't believe that money is ever free. And we can know what people believed about the situation by just observing their behavior. If they thought that it was possible to get free money, we can assume that they would not have walked by, ignoring the opportunity to get some. So the meaning they attached and what they experienced corresponded to their belief that "free money" isn't possible or nobody gives away money on the street—no strings attached. In fact, most people probably thought he was crazy, which would explain why people went out of their way to walk around him to avoid contact.

However, the environment was expressing itself in exactly the way in which it was representing itself. The sign reading "free money" was the truth, but the information "free money" did not connect with anything in anyone's mental environment so that it could be perceived as the truth. There was a direct one-to-one relationship between what any given individual believed, what he perceived, and what he experienced. Except for one man, everyone else obviously did not believe in the possibility of free money; they probably perceived a crazy man and thus had an erroneous experience relative to the conditions. Now, the environment did not choose the meaning any of these people placed on the information it was offering. And if the environment did not choose, then each individual created his own experience out of the situation that was presented to him. There were a number of alternate experiences available and each alternate experience would correspond to the type of belief someone would have about the possibilities.

BELIEFS

Beliefs create definitions, make distinctions, and shape our perception of environmental information by programming our senses to hear, see, and select information that corresponds with what we believe. Our experience of the environment will correspond to the choices we make, and these choices will correspond to the information that is perceivable. What is perceivable to each individual, however, may not have much of a relationship to what is available or possible from the environment's perspective. Each person in the illustration of free money would claim that what he experienced was, in fact, the true reality of the situation. What would cause them to believe anything different? People think of their beliefs and subsequent experiences as a fact of reality instead of a belief about reality. This is natural because beliefs create a relationship with the environment that is best described as circular or a closed loop.

What I mean by a closed loop is that every component part in the process of how we experience the environment supports every other component, making everything seem self-evident or beyond question. These closed-loop systems that beliefs create are extremely difficult to open up. The belief controls the information coming into the mental system, the information that is actually perceived will be consistent with the belief, the course of action taken will be consistent with the information perceived, and the subsequent experience will support and reinforce the validity of the belief. This is a closed system that will not allow for the possibility of other alternatives because the experiences keep on reinforcing the beliefs, making the beliefs seem increasingly more self-evident and beyond question. Unless we are open or even know how to be open to new information that could lead to new experiences, we will experience the closed-loop nature of our beliefs every moment, assuming the whole time that what we experienced in each situation was the only possibility available.

The people who walked by the man giving away free money didn't know they were completely oblivious to the possibility of the environment expressing itself in such a manner, even though the sign said "Free Money." And if confronted with the same set of environmental conditions again, they would behave the same way as the first time, not knowing that other distinctions are possible, even if they are remote. The perception and the experience have to match up because we can't experience something that we don't know about yet, unless we are open to the possibility that what we believe might be very limiting in relationship to what the environment is offering. Remember the man who refused to take the money even when it was being handed to him? He was being offered an experience that would have increased the number of distinctions he could make about the nature of the environment (free money does exist), and he would have grown mentally as a result. Being given free money was obviously a distinction he didn't know about yet. And even though it would seem that free money would be a powerful incentive to question one's belief that it doesn't exist, it wasn't enough for this man. His beliefs obviously did not allow him to even remotely consider the possibility, again creating this closed loop, leading him to believe that what he ended up with or experienced out of this situation was the true nature of his existence, when all it really was was a reflection of the true nature of his beliefs and how they manage environmental information.

Beliefs define the parameters in which we perceive environmental information. All definitions by definition create boundaries. Beliefs will manage information in various ways to maintain a balance between the inner and outer environment. Any perceived imbalance will result in some degree of either stress or illusion. In maintaining a balance, many of our responses to environmental conditions are automatic because our beliefs make the response seem self-evident, when, in fact, under any given set of environmental conditions alternate experiences exist along side of the experiences our beliefs locked us into.

By inhibiting the flow of information into the mental system, beliefs do exactly what they are supposed to do. They limit our awareness of data so that we can learn in stages. If we believe that things exist in only one particular way, then our beliefs will act as a natural mechanism to block the acceptance of any conflicting information.

Considering or accepting any new or conflicting information would open up choices that we ordinarily would not have to consider. Too many choices too soon can cause confusion and mental overload. If it were not for the limiting nature of beliefs, what would happen to our minds would probably be similar to what it would be like if a television set picked up all the information being broadcast from all the TV stations and projected that information on to the screen simultaneously on the same channel. Beliefs allow us to tune into one channel of environmental information at a time so that we can learn about the nature of the environment through that one channel. Then we can expand our awareness to pick up another channel as we learn how to deal with the additional choices we are confronted with as we become aware of the additional possibilities.

HOW OUR FEARS FUNCTION TO CREATE THE EXPERIENCE WE ARE TRYING TO AVOID

What we perceive is a function of the distinctions that we have learned to make. What we focus our attention on—out of all the distinctions we have learned to perceive—is a function of the intensity of the energy in the perception loop. We only have so much of our conscious attention to give to whatever information happens to be available in any given moment. Fear (high degree of negatively charged energy) has a profoundly limiting effect on the range of information that we can pay attention to. It causes us to narrow our range of perception to focus our attention on to the object of our fears. How else could we avoid what we perceive as threatening?

Learning to drive is an excellent example that illustrates how fear narrows our focus of attention. The dangers of driving are obvious even to someone who has never driven before. It isn't too difficult to imagine the harmful effects of a head-on collision. Without having developed the necessary skills to control the car, the new driver would lack the confidence to know that he can respond appropriately to any given situation. That is, he doesn't trust himself. As a result, he will feel some degree of uncomfortableness or fear when he drives. The fear will, in turn, cause him to focus his attention on the oncoming traffic or concentrate on the eye/hand coordination necessary to keep the car in the appropriate lane. Because he is so focused on what he can't do and what may happen as a result, he has little if any of his attention available to do anything else, like carry on a conversation with a passenger, notice the scenery in his peripheral vision, or even read road signs. All this other environmental information is available and perceivable, but in his case it is either blocked or unnoticed because he has to devote so much of his attention to the object of his fear (the lack of control he has over the car). At the point where he becomes comfortable with his ability to drive safely, his field of awareness will open up allowing him to perceive all this other information.

The purpose of fear is to help us avoid those things in the environment we have learned to perceive as threatening. However, when we couple our painful memories with our natural propensity to associate and group environmental components together—instead of avoiding the object of our fears—we will actually create the very experiences we are trying to avoid. For example, a child severely bitten by a dog will quite naturally associate all dogs with the threat of pain and consequently generate an intense fear or even terror whenever he encounters any dog in the future. The child's fear of all other dogs other than the one that bit him is real. He has no way of making a distinction between a friendly and a dangerous dog because his personal experience has taught him that all dogs are dangerous. Because of this natural propensity to associate, all we need is one first-time experience to believe that all dogs are dangerous. That is his truth about the nature of the environment. However, his truth is not all the environment has to offer in the way of experiences in relationship to dogs. Not every dog that exists is dangerous. Quite the contrary, very few would be considered threatening; most see a child and want to play.

Now, in every chance encounter the child has with a dog in the future he will create an experience of terror, regardless of the disposition of any particular dog he happens to run into. If a dog makes any movement toward the child, the child will perceive that movement as an actual attack when all the dog wanted to do was play or be petted. In fact, the child could become so afraid of being attacked that he will devote most if not all of his attention to scanning the surrounding environment for dogs. Eventually his senses will become attuned to picking up their sights and sounds. And every time he sees or hears one, he will create another terrifying experience that just reinforces his fears. His focus of attention will attract to his attention the object of his fears so that he can avoid what he has learned is threatening. The problem is that what he has learned is erroneous in relationship to the conditions, that not all dogs are dangerous. Not knowing that, he will naturally believe that his terror is coming from outside him instead of inside him. In effect his fears are acting on his perception to create the very experiences he is trying to avoid by causing him to hone in on all the dogs in the environment.

What we focus our attention on in the environment is what we will usually get. The dog-biting example is a graphic illustration of this. However, there are other ways that our fears act as a cause to create what we are trying to avoid that aren't so obvious. Remember that all fears act on our perception as a warning mechanism to help us avoid what we believe to be threatening. One way to avoid the object of our fears is simply to refuse to acknowledge the existence of threatening information. Another more subtle way that will create some real blind spots in our perception is to focus all our attention on alternative—nonthreatening—information to the exclusion of everything else. These blind spots will exclude whole categories of perceivable information from our awareness, which can result in some disastrous consequences, especially in the trading environment.

For example, let's say that the market is offering us what we believe to be a good opportunity to make some money, so we go ahead and put on a trade, but at the same time we are also operating out of a fear of being wrong. We will fear being wrong because, if we are, it will force us to feel whatever negative energy has accumulated inside of us as a result of being wrong in the past. Now, if the market offers us a choice between information that would indicate we are right or information that would indicate that we are wrong, what information will we naturally focus our attention on? The information that will make us right, without acknowledging or considering the implications of the information that would indicate otherwise. Again, those implications could be disastrous.

Let's look at another example of a trader who is afraid of losing. A fear of losing presents an obvious conflict because it would be difficult to put on a trade in the first place. However, for the sake of this example, let's say this trader was so attracted to a specific opportunity that he managed to operate outside of his fear long enough to put on a trade. Now, the kind of information he focuses his attention on will depend on what the market does. If the market goes against him, he will be afraid to confront the possibility of another loss, so he will focus his attention on any other nonthreatening information. If the market happens to come back to his entry point, he will exit the trade in a sigh of relief, regardless of what the potential is for any further movement in his direction. But, if the market continues to go against him, his mental defenses will begin to break down as the threatening information becomes just too overwhelming for him to be able to block from his awareness any longer. At that point he could easily become paralyzed and not be able to do anything on his behalf. Eventually his stress and anxiety will become so acute that the only way he can relieve it is by getting out of the trade.

On the other hand, if he finds himself in a winning trade he will focus on completely different information. His fear of losing will cause him to focus his attention on what the market can take away from him. In a winning trade he will exclude from his awareness any information that would indicate what the potential is for the market to continue to move in his direction, which is the only information he focused on in a losing trade, and instead focus exclusively on information that will confirm his fears of the market, retracing back to his entry point or beyond. In effect, his fear of losing causes him to exit the trade early for a small profit regardless of whatever the possible profit potential was in that trade. Once he is out, if the market continues to move in his original direction, he will agonize over the profits he left on the table and wonder why he just couldn't hang in there just a little longer, not realizing that his fear of losing actually caused him to lose all those additional profits.

What you have just been given is an example of why the vast majority of traders cut their profits short and let their losses run. In a winning trade, the fear of losing will cause us to focus our attention on information that the market is going to take our profits away, compelling us to get out early. In a losing trade we will focus our attention on just the opposite information—anything other than that which would indicate the trade is a loser. Fear causes us to act without a perception of choice. When we are afraid to confront certain categories of market information, it drastically limits the choices that we perceive as available. Cutting a loss isn't a choice if we systematically block from our awareness any information that would indicate that we are in a losing trade. Staying in a winner isn't a choice if we are consumed with the fear that the market is going to take away our money.

To prevent these blind spots in our perception, we have to learn to trade without fear. And to trade without fear we need to completely trust ourselves to confront and accept whatever information the market is offering about itself, and we need to be able to trust ourselves to know that we will always act in our best interests without hesitation, regardless of the conditions. Any endeavor will require some degree of trust. We would find it difficult to cross the street it we didn't trust ourselves to be able to get out of the way of the oncoming traffic. From a psychological perspective, the market environment can wreak just as much havoc in our lives as getting hit by a car. To be successful as traders, we need to believe that we can win with an absence of fear so we can make better assessments of the conditions and perceive more choices. What this means is that we have to do the necessary mental work to release ourselves from anything within us that would cause us to narrow our focus of attention or specifically block certain categories of information from our awareness.

CHAPTER 11

Why We Need to Learn How to Adapt

There is a direct relationship between our ability to adapt to changing environmental conditions and the level of satisfaction we feel about our lives. To adapt to the changes occurring in the outside environment implies that we are changing ourselves as we learn more and more of what the environment has to offer in terms of distinctions about its nature. The more distinctions we can make between the various components of the environment and how they act as a force on one another, the more information becomes available to us through our perception. As we expand our perception of information available, we will gain a deeper level of understanding and insight into the cause-and-effect relationship that we have with the outside environment, that is, how the environment has the potential to act as a force on us and how the environment will react to the force of our behavior.

The deeper the level of our understanding and insight, the more effectively we can interact with the environment to fulfill our needs and achieve our goals. Fulfilling our needs and achieving our goals create within us a feeling of well-being, confidence, and satisfaction about our lives that would otherwise be characterized by feelings of dissatisfaction, disappointment, and deterioration when we can't fulfill ourselves. Success, confidence, and satisfaction are all synonymous. They breed from one another to create and perpetuate a positive cycle of expansion and mental growth. And, by the same token, disappointment, dissatisfaction, and deterioration also feed on one another to create negative cycles of emotional pain, anxiety, and depression.

To fulfill our needs and achieve our goals, there has to be some level of correspondence or balance between the inner mental environment and the outer physical environment. What I mean by "correspondence" is some level of understanding of how the outer environment works. Our needs, intents, goals, and desires—all— exist first in the mental environment. Then one of three things can happen in some future moment in the physical environment; they are either 100 percent fulfilled, partially fulfilled, or not fulfilled at all, resulting in feelings of satisfaction or dissatisfaction equivalent to the degree of fulfillment.

To fulfill ourselves, we need to interact with the outside environmental forces. The extent to which we fulfill ourselves is a function of knowing the most appropriate set of steps to take in relationship to the outer conditions and to what extent we can act on what we know. Knowing the most appropriate set of steps to take in relationship to the prevailing conditions is a function of how much or little we have learned in relationship to what is available to be learned.

Example: Draw a large circle with a diameter of approximately 6 feet. This circle will represent everything that is available to be learned about the nature of the universe, not limited by what we know of it, but as it exists in every way as yet to be discovered. Now, draw a smaller circle within the larger one, with a diameter of approximately 2 feet. This smaller circle will represent all the accumulated knowledge of humankind since the dawn of our existence, in other words, what we have learned in relationship to what we have yet to discover about the interacting forces of our environment and ourselves. Now, place a dot within the smaller circle. This dot would probably be a fair representation of what each of us as individuals has accumulated in knowledge, insight, and understanding, in relationship to what has already been discovered and learned by others (both in the past and present), in relationship to everything else that is still waiting to be discovered.

The empty space between the inside boundaries of the larger circle and the smaller circle is basically everything we don't know or haven't learned about yet, either individually or collectively. There are many things in the environment available to be experienced. However, until we learn about them, we won't experience them, just as people couldn't experience atomic energy until it was discovered. Yet it existed in the environment, waiting to be experienced and learned about for hundreds of thousands of years before we actually discovered it. These were hidden components that had to be actively uncovered by someone. Otherwise, if the environment acts as a force on us in ways that we haven't learned to understand yet, we will either dismiss the experience as not real or form some superstition or think of it as some unknown or random force, until we investigate and understand the phenomena. When we investigate, we learn to make enough distinctions to recognize all the interacting components acting as a force on one another to create the effect that we also believed was random, until we learned about the experience. For years, many people in the academic community believed that the markets were random; this is a perfect example of their general lack of understanding of human nature. People act as a force on prices in perfectly logical ways, when you understand the logic of their fears.

The small circle represents what has been discovered and experienced by somebody at sometime in human history. All the discoveries throughout human history have expanded the small circle to include more and more of the larger one. For example, the small circle would probably have been a tenth of its present size during the Middle Ages. Each discovery since then changed the environment that we could experience because it added something to the mental environment that didn't previously exist in it. In other words, as we learned, we changed the way we perceived the world around us, resulting in the evolution of the thinking of humankind overall.

There is no question that the accumulated knowledge of humankind has increased to levels that would be completely inconceivable to or boggle the mind of even the broadest, most progressive thinking person alive just 100 years ago. Everything that exists now that didn't exist then (cars, planes, phones, computers, etc.) is the result of what someone learned and shared with others, and consequently it changed the consistency and makeup of the environment we live in. And yet all of what we have now existed as possibilities since the beginning of humankind. The possibility for manned space flight existed from the first moment that a person looked up into a star-lit sky and wondered what it would be like to be on the moon. Of course, we didn't even attempt to do it until our knowledge evolved to a point where mere wishing could be turned into a reality. But what if we could go back to 1889 and tell the typical 40-year-old person about the world their great, great, great-grandchildren will grow up in? There is no way he would believe how different things will be. He wouldn't believe it because he wouldn't have the mental framework to believe it, just like we would have a very difficult time believing what we will have evolved into 100 years from now.

The dot simply represents the world we experience as individuals in relationship to what would be possible to experience if we had inside of our mental environment all the accumulated knowledge of humankind. Everything you and I know as individuals in relationship to everything we haven't learned yet would represent the current set of limitations that we operate from. That is, all our individual accumulated knowledge—every memory, belief, distinction, association, insight, or understanding—about the nature of the physical environment would all represent our personal limitations compared to what is available in the environment to experience, believe, and understand. That is, there will always be more information available in the environment than what our personal limitations will allow us to perceive or experience.

Just contemplate the immensity of what we don't know yet; consider that every person who exists acts as a force on the environment to change it in some way that can affect us as individuals in some gratifying or unsatisfying way. The way in which each individual acts as a cause to change the environment, which in turn, affects everyone else, will correspond to the makeup of his mental environment. So, until you or I understand every facet of everyone else's behavior and the ways in which they can express themselves to act as a force on the environment (meaning the rest of us), then every other person that exists would represent an unknown outside force to the extent that we haven't learned about human nature or understand it.

We could start filling in the small circle with dots to represent the knowledge of each individual that exists on the planet, until the circle was almost filled. The blank space left in the small circle would represent knowledge that exists in some form that is not inside the mind of some person alive today. We could also organize the dots into clusters, where each dot would overlap a bit to represent the shared knowledge and beliefs of different cultures, although they couldn't overlap too much because we all know something different because of our individual differences in experiences. The dots would also have to be different sizes to represent the increased or decreased levels of understanding and insight that we operate out of in relationship to one another. For example, the dot of a child would be much smaller than the dot of a typical adult.

The physical environment was here before we were born—and we certainly weren't born with the insight that we need to interact with it in such a way that we can assure ourselves of experiencing high levels of satisfaction. For example, if there was a 100 percent correspondence between our mental and physical environment, then everything there is to know about the nature of the physical environment we would have already learned, and this knowledge would be a component part of the mental environment. Implied within this perfect correspondence would be a complete understanding of all the forces that operate in the physical environment, coupled with a complete understanding of their cause-and-effect relationship. We would know exactly how the environment would act as a force on us to create experience and how the environment would respond as a counteracting force to the force we apply to it through our behavior. And, therefore, with this perfect understanding we would know the most appropriate set of steps to take to fulfill our needs, intents, goals, and desires, resulting in a complete state of satisfaction. I am defining behavior as the outward physical expression of mental energy acting as a force on the outside environment.

Obviously, none of us possesses this kind of perfect correspondence with the environment, and, as a result, it is probably safe to say that none of us lives our lives in a complete state of satisfaction. However, the more we understand and know about the interacting forces behind our own behavior and the interacting environmental forces outside of us, the easier it is to fulfill our needs and achieve our goals, resulting in greater levels of satisfaction that we will experience in our lives. Conversely, if we don't understand our own behavior, we certainly can't begin to understand or anticipate anyone else's, and the less we understand and know about the rest of the environmental components that have a potential to act as a force on us, then it would stand to reason that the less potential we have to fulfill our needs and achieve our goals, resulting in feelings of disappointment, stress, anxiety, unhappiness, and fear.

LEARNING AND
THE QUALITY OF OUR EXPERIENCES

As I have mentioned, we aren't born with the knowledge that we need to operate effectively in the physical environment to fulfill ourselves. However, we are born with the need to know. This need to know operates as a driving force in our lives coming from the innermost depths of who we are. Our natural sense of curiosity compels us to explore and learn. For example, once we have learned the nature of something or accomplished some task, we quickly become bored and go on to something different. Boredom acts as an inner force compelling us to look for something new to discover and learn about.

Attractions also act as an inner force, compelling us to move through the environment to discover and create experience. Take the object of a child's curiosity (something he is attracted to) away from him and what will happen? He will usually start crying or even throw a fit. His crying is an indication that his inner needs are not being fulfilled. Crying is a form of grieving to compensate for the lack of balance between the inner and outer environments. When we have explored the object of our attraction to our satisfaction, it means the inside has been filled with what the outside has to offer in terms of experience. When that happens we simply lose interest, become bored, and start to scan the environment for something else that might attract our attention.

There is another characteristic of our nature that supports our need to learn. Whenever we learn a skill, the steps involved in the operation of that skill drop down to an unconscious level of operation, so we are then free to learn something new. To learn a skill, we usually have to break the skill down into a series of small steps and concentrate on each individual step until we can put all the steps together into a series of effective movements. By concentrating on each small step, we narrow our focus of attention to the point where we are oblivious to anything else going on in the environment. For example, think of a time in your life when you were tying to learn a new skill, say, in some sport, and while you were trying to put all the movements together, someone was attempting to get your attention on some completely unrelated matter. In such a situation we would find it extremely difficult, if not impossible, to stay focused on one without destroying our concentration on the other. However, after we have successfully made the skill a learned resource, we could easily perform the movements while focusing our attention elsewhere.

Without this characteristic of our nature, where our skills drop to an unconsciousness level of operation, we would find it nearly impossible to move beyond the performance level of a typical infant. Just think what it would be like if we had to concentrate on all the movements necessary just to pick something up the way a typical infant does. We didn't always have the eye/hand coordination that we take completely for granted. We had to learn it. We learned it because we were attracted to things in the environment we wanted to experience with our sense of touch. As we learn each skill, we can automatically access the series of movements to execute the skill so we don't have to concentrate on any of the individual steps, which then frees our attention to explore and continually expand what we can become aware of.

Learning is a function of our existence. It will occur quite naturally through our powerful sense of curiosity and what we find ourselves attracted to in the environment that we just need to know everything about. At the most fundamental level, learning will happen just because we are alive and have to interact with the environment to stay alive. So we will learn something. However, that doesn't necessarily mean that what we have learned is very useful with respect to how we might go about fulfilling ourselves in some satisfactory way. We have very little control in our early years over what we learn about the nature of the outside world and how it works. I will discuss this in more detail in a moment.

As we expand our personal dot (as in the example) to learn more and more of what the environment has to offer in the way of insight about itself, we increase our level of correspondence with it. When we learn, we change the makeup and consistency of our inner environment. Each change we make on the inside simultaneously changes our perspective and perception of the outside. The outside environment is different because we are operating out of new insights and understandings as a result of what has been added to or changed on the inside. Each new insight makes available to us new and different choices on how to interact more appropriately with the environment to change the quality of our experiences.

This may seem like an obvious correlation between what we have learned and how much satisfaction we experience in our lives, but I assure you it is not. If it was so obvious, then most people wouldn't have such a difficult time making the connection between the deteriorating conditions, lack of happiness or satisfaction in their lives and their lack of insight, coupled with a refusal to acknowledge there is something they don't know and need to learn.

There are always greater levels of satisfaction available in every experience until we reach the point where we know everything there is to know. If we did know everything there is to know, we could expect outcomes from the outside that would correspond exactly with the inside mental environment. This kind of perfect correspondence between inner and outer would be the result of our perfect understanding of ourselves—the inner forces that act on our behavior—in relationship to the outer environmental forces that act on us. Since none of us is at the level of perfect knowledge, we can assume that within every experience we have with the physical environment there are other probable experiences resulting from other choices that were available but unknown to us at the time, the point being that what we end up with in any given situation will correspond exactly with our level of understanding, insight, and ability to act on what we know.

The more we allow ourselves to learn, the better able we are at making assessments about the possibilities that exist in some future moment. However, implied within the foregoing statement is that we are, first, willing to acknowledge that other possible futures exist, not just the one future that our expectations and beliefs about what we have already learned lock us into. Keep in mind that everything we know in relationship to everything we haven't learned yet would represent the current set of limitations that we operate out of. Conceptually, these individual limitations are no different from the choices people in the Middle Ages were blinded to by believing that the Earth was flat.

If we aren't willing to acknowledge that in any given situation more information and choices exist than what our beliefs allow us to perceive, then we will never learn to recognize or anticipate the existence of these other more satisfying possibilities. By acknowledging the possibility that a more appropriate set of steps exists, we open ourselves up to perceive and then learn the steps that can lead to greater levels of satisfaction. Refusing to acknowledge the existence of these possibilities would be the same as claiming that electricity didn't exist before it was discovered. When we continually argue for the status quo by defending what we already believe we know, the environment will seem to be constantly assaulting us, resulting in feelings of stress and anxiety. The outer environment becomes assaulting because it is offering us more to learn about the nature of the ways in which things exist and we are simply refusing to learn.

In fact, we can easily determine if we need to learn something to operate in the environment more effectively by just monitoring the way we feel. If there were never an imbalance or lack of correspondence between the mental and the physical environments, then theoretically we wouldn't ever have a reason to feel disappointment, frustration, confusion, stress, or anxiety. It is only because there is an imbalance, a lack of harmony or correspondence, between the mental and physical that we ever experience any of these unpleasant, negative emotions. Because when there is a balance between the inside and outside, we experience the opposite feelings of joy, happiness, and satisfaction. So it would stand to reason that any time we feel these negative emotions, it is because we either didn't know the most appropriate set of steps, resulting in frustration and disappointment, or we don't know what to do next, resulting in stress, anxiety, and confusion. *In any case, our feelings will always tell us about the state of our relationship with the environment and point the way to what we need to learn to experience greater degrees of satisfaction.*

For example, if we aren't experiencing satisfaction in our personal relationships, would it be too simple to assume that the reason is because we haven't developed the appropriate interpersonal skills? Is it possible that there are certain communication skills available that—once learned and used—can result in much more satisfying personal relationships and deeper levels of intimacy? The problem is that it is just as easy to assume that the appropriate skills leading to greater levels of satisfaction don't exist or that we already know what we need to know and if we aren't experiencing satisfaction now, it must therefore not be possible to experience it at all. When we operate out of the last assumption, even if the environment presents us with evidence that deeper levels of satisfaction are possible (observing another couple who are experiencing satisfaction), we would probably assume that they are acting as if they were happy for appearance's sake. That way, we won't have to take responsibility for learning something they might know.

The first assumption would result in investigation, learning, and expansion, leading to greater levels of effectiveness and satisfaction. The last two assumptions would obviously lead to more dissatisfaction. The names and places may change, but we will experience the same kind of painful conditions over and over again. These cycles of dissatisfaction will continue until we acknowledge there is something we need to learn and go about the task of learning it.

WHAT WE ALREADY KNOW WILL BLOCK
WHAT WE HAVEN'T LEARNED YET

Obviously, acknowledging there is something that we need to learn is not as easy as it sounds. In fact, acknowledging that we don't know something or that what we do know isn't very useful or effective presents us with one of the major paradoxes of life. The dilemma we are confronted with is how can we know what we don't know when what we have already learned will block our perception of what we haven't learned yet. For example, once we learn that trading is easy (the first few quick winning trades will establish that belief), it will block our perception of information to the contrary, that trading is probably one of the hardest endeavors one could choose to undertake. Each of these beliefs—that trading is easy or trading is hard—would result in the perception of completely different choices as being available from the environment, resulting in very different outcomes based on the choices perceived and acted on.

We don't question the usefulness or effectiveness of something we have already learned, simply because what each of us has learned we experienced in some way. That is, we won't question what we have experienced just because we experienced it, meaning the reality of the experience is based in our five senses: what is inside of us we either, felt, saw, heard, smelled, or tasted. That's real enough. Once an experience becomes a component part of our mental environment in the form of a memory, belief, or association, it becomes a part of what is commonly believed to be our identity and beyond question.

However, we are open to learn practically anything the environment has to offer, if we haven't been previously exposed in some way. We will soak up first-time information like a sponge, regardless of what it is. However, once it is inside of us, we will either defend it or defend against it (hide from information in the environment that we don't want to acknowledge as a part of our mental environment), instead of making ourselves available to learn more of what the environment has to offer in the way of insight about itself or ourself as the case may be.

To defend against the intrusion of information requires energy. This investment in energy is commonly referred to as stress. The simplest definition that I can think of for stress is that it is what we feel when we are actively blocking information from the environment. In physical terms stress is really no different from walking against the wind. Symbolically, the wind would represent various categories of environmental information we don't want to confront; our bodies walking against the wind would represent what we have already learned—what is already inside of us that blocks what is outside of us. The two forces clash and we feel stress.

One of the biggest ironies of life is that everyone wants to be right. In other words, everyone assumes what they have experienced and learned about the nature of the way things exist to be the true and correct version. The irony is everyone's version is correct by virtue of the fact that what is inside all of us was experienced by our physical senses—if we saw it, if we read it, if we heard it, if we felt it, if we tasted it, if we smelled it, or any combination thereof, we experienced it. However, not everybody's version (of what the environment has to offer in the way of experiences) is particularly useful or effective as a resource for interacting with the environment in a way that would lead to satisfactory outcomes. Just because something gets input into our mental environment doesn't mean that it's of any real value in helping us to fulfill ourselves.

A child has no way of conceptualizing how his experiences are forming beliefs about the nature of reality, concepts that would, in fact, be much different under different environmental conditions.

He unquestioningly takes an experience as a fact of reality because the beliefs he is forming are founded in feelings and emotions. He does not reflect on his experiences to assess the quality of the beliefs he is forming. He has no way of determining how these beliefs will either act as resources or obstacles to self-expression in the future.

The child doesn't understand that any belief that he forms will define reality in a way that excludes other possibilities or that he will make associations with experiences, lumping components of the environment together in ways that are very limiting and not practical. Many of these beliefs will just naturally be decharged as his attractions cause him to interact with the environment in new ways. All of us will just naturally grow into a new set of limitations as we expand our awarenesses by learning, which in turn releases us from things we used to believe. However, if the quality of the energy in many of our beliefs is negatively charged, then our fear will act as an obstacle to self-expression, limiting what we can perceive from the environment as possibilities.

For example, someone who grew up constantly being belittled or criticized by his parents knows exactly how that feels. The beliefs he forms about himself and his relationship with the environment, as a result, were formed in a reality of pain. Certainly he wouldn't know, while growing up, that he was forming a belief about his relative unworthiness as a person. Unworthiness is a concept that he may not learn about well into his adult years, and he may never learn how to release himself from the damaging effects. But in the meantime, his fear of being ridiculed and belittled will drastically limit the possibilities he perceives in the environment for self-expression. Many possibilities that seem self-evident to someone without this fear would be totally out of the realm of possibility for him.

An even bigger irony is that the more we acknowledge the possibility that our version of the way things exist isn't as effective of a resource as it could be, the more we make ourselves available to learn from the environment. By expanding our personal dot to include more of what is outside of us inside of us, the more it increases our level of correspondence with the outside, leaving less and less of what is out there that we don't know about, thereby increasing our ability to be right.

The more we allow ourselves to learn, the better able we are at making assessments about the probabilities that exist in some future moment. How could we not be better off by learning something when you consider that the environment can act as a force on us in an almost infinite variety of ways, some of which we know about, many others we couldn't begin to anticipate unless we keep on learning in spite of what we already know? The more we believe we know, the more we make the environment prove to us that what we know isn't particularly useful or effective. The problem is that proof could be right in front of our noses and we wouldn't have the mental framework to recognize it, unless we willingly allowed ourselves to confront it and consider it. Otherwise, if we all knew so much, we wouldn't ever experience emotional pain, because it is a perfect indication that we don't know how to interact with the environment to our satisfaction—because if we did, we would.

All this should be somewhat apparent because it is not a typical human characteristic to actively gather and consider information that conflicts with what we already know and believe to be true. However, consider that hidden within the environmental information that we haven't learned to perceive yet, either because we haven't learned to make the appropriate distinctions or because the information is being blocked by our current set of beliefs, are a more appropriate set of steps to fulfilling ourselves. What we haven't learned yet is outside of each one of us waiting to become a part of our personal dot. What we don't know represents all the information that could result in choices that have much more satisfying outcomes. However, since we can't know what we haven't learned yet and what we do know blocks the perception of other alternatives that exist for satisfaction, we easily get caught in these terribly unsatisfying life cycles, believing that is all the world has to offer, when our predicament is merely the result of our inability to adapt ourselves. When we do allow ourselves to adapt, we learn that there are always more choices available than our beliefs will allow us to perceive. What I mean by adapt is to identify and actively change something that is already inside of us so there is a higher degree of correspondence between the inside and outside.

Each first-time experience with the physical environment creates a distinction in the mental environment about its nature. All information or possibilities that exist in the same category as that first experience will then be filtered perceptually through what we learned from that experience. Again I will use the example of a child whose first experience with a dog is a painful one, meaning that the first dog the child attempted to play with, out of his natural sense of curiosity, bit him. As a result of this one experience the child will "naturally associate" all dogs with the one that bit him. What he learned will then act as a mental barrier to anything else the environment may have to offer with respect to all other dogs.

I have used the words "naturally associate" to point out that the child will not have to actively think about the limiting way in which dogs will be characterized in his mental environment. The associations will occur automatically, as a natural function of the way our minds are wired. So he will not have to see "the" dog that bit him; any dog will cause him to remember the pain of his previous experience. As a result of his first experience with a dog being painful, he will automatically associate any future encounters with dogs with his one painful experience. Regardless of how erroneous his association is or how the environment may try to prove to him that most dogs are friendly and will not cause him pain, he won't believe it, because what he has already learned about dogs (not one dog, but all dogs) will cause him to block the acceptance of this new information into his mental system.

However, if the child's first experience with a dog is positive, he will obviously have no reservations to play with any dog until he has a painful experience. In this case, however, if he is bitten, he will not automatically associate all other dogs with the one that bit him because he has already learned that the environment has more to offer than this one painful experience. What he will learn, that is new for him, is that not all dogs are friendly and that he must use some caution when interacting with them until he can determine their disposition.

The child whose first experience was painful doesn't know that he can experience happiness and joy with dogs. He doesn't know it because he hasn't experienced it; it isn't something he has learned yet, regardless of the evidence the environment may be presenting him. Nor will he likely learn it until he is willing to step through his fear. All other information being offered to him about the nature of dogs will be blocked or rejected by the energy of what he has already learned.

You can teach a child anything you please, regardless of how erroneous or dysfunctional it is relative to the environmental conditions. The child will believe what you teach him because what he experiences becomes a part of his identity. Anything we experience will become a functioning part of our identity. When I say "functioning," I mean that once something is inside of us, regardless of what it is, it then has the potential to act as a force on our behavior. All these functioning parts that we call memories of experiences, beliefs, and associations, in turn then act as an internal force to shape our perception of the environment we experience out of what is available to experience.

As you already know, what each one of us fears as individuals is something that we have at some point in our lives learned to fear, as a result of our experiences. When we feel fear, it is because we have learned to perceive the environmental conditions as threatening in some way, whereas someone who hasn't had a painful experience associated with those same environmental conditions has learned to perceive the environment conditions in a completely different way, a way that corresponds with his previous experience. One person can perceive the conditions as a threat, the other as an opportunity, in the same moment, based on what is already inside of them. In other words, what they have already taken into their mental environment as experience will determine how they perceive the environmental conditions, whether as an opportunity to experience joy or as a threat to experience pain and all the degrees in between. What is really interesting is that neither one would be able to convince the other of the validity of his perception, because what they are experiencing at the moment is directly related to what they have already learned.

We will usually only question the value of something that is inside of us, if we are forced to, as an absolute last resort. What would be the ultimate proof that we need to finally make us acknowledge that there is something we need to learn? Pain! We will acknowledge the need to learn when we are experiencing the emotional pain of a great disappointment or stress and anxiety because we don't know what to do next, and we are finding it increasingly difficult to shift the responsibility for what we are ending up with.

If we go back to the "believing that trading is easy" example, why would we consider that trading is difficult when we already know that it is easy? What would cause us to question the usefulness of such a belief? The emotional pain of disappointment as a result of not being able to achieve our goals? Once we question the usefulness, what happens? A whole world of information opens up to us on how we can learn to interact with the trading environment more effectively by increasing our level of correspondence. However, everything we would find in the environment to increase our understanding already existed, unless we think of something completely new on our own. The only thing that stopped us from finding it before was the energy of what we already knew, blocking what we haven't learned yet. The problem is that if learning something new means that we have to change what we have already learned, we instinctively seem to refuse to do it, regardless of how inappropriate what we have learned may be relative to what we would need to know to experience satisfaction. Once we have learned something, it will act as a force to block other information that would result in the perception of other choices. Even children will resist the acceptance of information that is contrary to what they have already learned, regardless of how dysfunctional their knowledge may be.

All learning is synonymous with change, whether we are changing something we already know or learning something completely new. If we refuse to change (adapt) the inside—adding to what we know to create more distinctions and change our perspective—then we are not learning what we need to know to experience something different in the outer environment. If there is no change on the inside, there will be no perceived change in the outside, thereby locking us into recurring cycles of pain and dissatisfaction. What's more, we will continue to suffer until the pain becomes so great that we are left with no choice other than to reassess how we go about managing our lives, that is, reassessing the usefulness of our beliefs.

WHAT WE DO KNOW BECOMES OBSOLETE

Besides the cycles of dissatisfaction that our current set of limitations locks us into (what we know blocks what we haven't learned yet), there is an even more practical reason for learning how to adapt. All of us are forced to interact with a constantly changing physical environment to fulfill our needs and achieve our goals. The way we interact with the environment, what choices we perceive in relationship to what is actually available from the environment's perspective, and what we do in relationship to what we perceive are all a function of what we have learned. Now, if you will recall, everything that constitutes the physical environment is in constant motion. Anything that is in motion (which includes everything made of atoms and molecules) is also changing over time. So change is an automatic function of the physical environment.

However, the mental environment is composed of positively or negatively charged energy that carries information about our experiences, what we have learned that forms into organizational patterns that we call beliefs and concepts about the nature of the physical environment. Energy is not made of atoms and molecules and therefore does not change over time. In fact, energy exists in a nonphysical dimension outside of time as we perceive it with our senses. Electrical energy or chemically produced electrical energy can be stored just the same as in a battery and the information it carries is stored with it. That is, time has no effect on the quality of this energy (the degree of the positive or negative charge) and the ways in which it affects our perception of environmental information and how it acts as a force on our behavior.

Changing our mental environment to correspond with the constant external changes going on in the physical environment is not automatic. The information stored in our mental environment about the nature of the physical environment can remain unchanged for years or a lifetime, for that matter, regardless of how outdated, useless, or even harmful it may be. And furthermore this outdated knowledge will continue to act as a force on our behavior, causing us to interact with the environment in completely inappropriate ways relative to the conditions. So even if we are experiencing satisfaction in certain areas of our lives, we cannot take it for granted that the conditions that we have learned to interact with will stay as we know them to exist. The outside conditions are in constant motion, presenting us with different forces to learn about and adapt to. In the market environment, for example, the changes in conditions are highly visible and usually moment to moment, whereas in other types of environments that we typically operate in, the forces of change work a little slower and are less visible, but they are changing nevertheless. The problem is that the conditions will change and we won't necessarily recognize these changes even if we start to experience some degree of dissatisfaction, unless we are constantly vigilant that even though we have learned something that works, it can still become obsolete.

CHAPTER 12

The Dynamics of Goal Achievement

The extent to which we fulfill our needs and achieve our goals with any degree of satisfaction is, first, a function of our being able to recognize our needs and formulate our goals. This is not as simple as it sounds. Our natural sense of curiosity and our attractions are very powerful inner forces that create a state of need or put us in a state of imbalance with the physical environment until the needs are satisfied. When we feel these attractions to certain activities, people, or objects in the environment, it is often difficult to visualize the possibilities or formulate any plans because of other inner forces in the form of beliefs, associations, or memories that act as barriers. We need to understand the relationship and possible conflicts between what we need or feel very attracted to and these other inner forces that in a sense say no.

The extent to which we fulfill our needs and achieve our goals with any degree of satisfaction is, second, a function of the degree to which we understand the nature of the external environmental forces we have to interact with to fulfill our needs and achieve our goals. (The depth of our understanding will correlate directly with the way in which we express ourselves in the environment to create the effect that we want.) Third, it is a function of the repertoire of skills that we have developed to interact with the environment and, fourth, a function of our ability to execute those skills.

Any differences between what we wanted, expected, desired, or needed and what we got is simply an indication of the degree to which we haven't learned what we needed to know or evidence that we don't have the appropriate skills to do what needed to be done. Included as a factor in the first category—where we haven't learned what we needed to know—is our ability or lack thereof to objectively (without illusion) assess the availability of what we wanted or needed from the environment's perspective. In other words, what we wanted may have not been available to begin with or available in the quantity we wanted or in the time frame we wanted or needed, and we didn't have the mental framework to make the kinds of distinctions to indicate the actual availability beforehand.

We also have to consider that what we wanted may have actually been available but unperceivable, as a result of not having learned to make the appropriate distinctions, which would, in turn, give us the kind of perspective where we could notice its availability. In these kinds of situations we usually end up saying to ourselves, "I wish," or "If only I had known that then," when we find out afterward what we didn't know at the time would have made a difference on how we "saw" things. Often, however, we never find out that what we wanted and didn't get was only one minor shift in perspective. Not knowing, of course, that the reason why we didn't get it was because we just didn't know there was something more we needed to learn. If we had the mental framework to make the appropriate distinctions, we can assume that we would have, unless something was blocking our perception.

I might add here that when we interact with other people, if we use force and manipulation to get what otherwise would be unavailable, what we are doing is forcing them to behave outside of their beliefs. If their beliefs were consistent with what we wanted from them, then we wouldn't need to use force or manipulation because a state of harmony would exist. We don't need to use force or manipulation on someone to do something that they already believe in. Whenever we do, it creates a state of imbalance in them that they would normally rectify by some means of revenge that we would just have to deal with at some point in the future. As a general observation of the human condition that goes along with this, most of us spend our lives trying to change what is in front of us to suit the makeup of our inner environment, when all we need to do is change the way we think about what is in front of us and we will change the quality of our experience of it.

In the second category—where we don't have the appropriate skills to do what needed to be done—we may recognize the most appropriate set of steps to take and also objectively assess the availability of what we want, but that doesn't mean that we have the skills to execute those steps. It is possible to underestimate the skills required in relation to the conditions to accomplish what we want (i.e., we don't know any better) or we could overestimate our abilities in relation to the conditions. Furthermore, even if we have learned the appropriate skills, there may be any number of beliefs or fears that act as barriers or limiting forces that will prevent us from properly executing the steps leading to what we want to accomplish. These beliefs or fears can be something that we have a conscious awareness of, or they can be completely subconscious. I am defining subconscious as any experience that we don't have immediate access to with our conscious thought process. For example, someone could be afraid of going into the water, be conscious of the fear itself, but not have the slightest recollection of a painful experience associated with water to know why he can't express himself in that way.

There is a very important distinction here that you need to make between recollection and memories. What we experience in the environment becomes a memory. Our ability to bring that memory into our conscious thought process is recollection. Some memories are easy to recall because the pathways to wherever the memory is stored are used a lot. In other words, we remember how to remember certain memories. However, there are many other experiences that become subconscious. These are memories that we have either forgotten how to remember because we don't use the pathways or we were never really fully aware of what was being perceived by our senses in the first place. However, the point here is that none of what goes in to the mental environment disappears or no longer exists just because we don't remember it. Our ability to recall consciously any particular belief that we are taught as a child or our ability to recall any particular experience is not a factor in the dynamics of how any of these mental components act as a force on our behavior. Neither is physical clock time for that matter. Our conscious recollection of experiences may fade with time, but time has no impact on the electrical charge (quality of energy) or the amount of emotional force behind the charge. For example, the old adage that time heals all wounds is not applicable to the mental environment. Time will heal wounds to the body because the body is a part of a physical reality where everything is in motion and changing over time. However, time has no impact on the memories stored in our mental environment because the mental environment is not composed of physical matter. It is composed of stored energy that does not change with the passing of time.

Emotional wounds (negatively charged mental energy) will never go away unless we learn how to release ourselves from them or change them. People think time heals emotional wounds, because after years of experiences they either inadvertently let go of the pain or build a system of beliefs as a defense to shield themselves from it. In fact, our seemingly infinite capacity to resist acknowledging the injury and hiding the effects of emotional wounds makes them very elusive. We almost always know when we have injured our bodies in some way. If you break your leg, you know it because you won't be able to walk. If it doesn't heal properly, you will know that too because you won't be able to walk the same as before or it may still hurt to walk. Yet, emotional wounds are not always so self-evident, because we can always structure our beliefs to make it seem as if we are not responsible for the cycles of dissatisfaction and emotional pain we experience in our lives, thus insulating ourselves from the effects of our own negatively charged energy.

This is being pointed out because I have found that most people have a great deal of difficulty believing that something that happened to them in their childhood can still affect how they perceive their environment and how they express themselves now. Although, when you think about it, how could it be any other way? Everything that we experience becomes a component part of our mental environment. All the parts then act as an inner cause, affecting how we experience the outside environment. Again, we don't have to be able to remember why we learned to be afraid of something to feel the fear. We don't even have to consciously acknowledge to ourselves that the fear exists because we can always rationalize that it is something else or use drugs or alcohol to block our awareness of it. However, regardless of how hard we try to stop ourselves from feeling what is inside of us, the feelings are still there; otherwise our efforts to block them wouldn't be necessary in the first place. The fear will exist because the energy, somewhere in our memory of some previous experience, will cause us to feel it, regardless of whether or not we allow ourselves to have a recollection of the source.

Memories, beliefs, and associations do not go away with time, substance abuse, or trying to put them somewhere in the subconscious that makes it more difficult to gain a conscious awareness. They will continue to act as a source of energy for the way in which we pick and choose information from the environment and how we express ourselves, for as long as we live, unless we learn how to manage them. Did you ever wonder why it was so difficult to break an unwanted habit or why it can be so difficult to execute some well-thought-out plan you were really committed to? It is difficult because of what is already inside of us that acts as resistance to our intent. An intent to do something is not necessarily a belief. In other words, out of everything we intend to do, some of those intentions will be supported by our beliefs, memories, and associations, and some will not. When there is support, our efforts will seem effortless, because there is no conflict between any beliefs, memories, and associations and what we intend to do. However, if our intents are not in harmony with our beliefs, memories, or associations, doing becomes a struggle, where we can't stay focused, become easily distracted, or make what most people would characterize as "stupid mistakes."

Take, for example, someone who smokes, decides it's a bad habit, and as a result, commits himself to quitting. Thus his intent is to express himself as a nonsmoker. However, after he has smoked his last cigarette, his beliefs in being a smoker will immediately start drawing his attention to cigarettes until it builds to the point where he craves a cigarette and then has one. What we have here is a classic conflict between an intent that is not only in conflict with other beliefs but the intent itself has no real structural support. That is, there isn't a corollary belief that says, "I am a nonsmoker." The energy for his behavior not to smoke will have to come from his conscious willingness to be a different person in this area of his life. However, his willingness doesn't instantly negate all the energy in the beliefs he has built up over the years in being a smoker. These beliefs will have a great deal of energy to act on his conscious attention (noticing cigarettes in the environment and thinking about cigarettes) and his behavior (to pick one up and smoke it).

We could even have inner support (beliefs, memories, and associations) for what we intend to do and still have difficulties following through with our plans because of other conflicting beliefs. Behavior that would fall into the "stupid mistake" category is most often the result of subconscious or forgotten beliefs that are in direct conflict with our intents. Trading is a perfect example to illustrate this. Many people devote a great deal of their time, energy, and financial resources to expressing themselves as traders. They learn a lot about trading—they are even highly regarded by their peers for what they know about the market—but still can't execute their trades properly or the way they planned. There are traders who can consistently make money day after day until they get to certain threshold levels and then promptly give all their profits back to the market in one or two trades. The way they give their money back is completely inconsistent with their trading style while they were making money. After they have lost a sufficient amount of money, they go back to the way they normally trade and start the process all over again. This kind of behavior is no accident. It happens for a reason.

In each of these situations these traders certainly had developed effective, workable strategies to be successful—they definitely had some highly structured beliefs to support their expression as a trader. However, what they haven't done is identify and decharge a whole host of other beliefs (both conscious and subconscious) that are in direct conflict with the endeavor of trading or making money as a trader. For example, there are many beliefs related to one's religious upbringing that are in direct conflict with the whole concept of speculating. And what is trading but taking money away from other traders with no services rendered? This kind of activity isn't consistent with most religious teachings. Another typical example is most people grow up with very powerful beliefs related to the work ethic. They have very rigid definitions about what constitutes work and how one earns one's money. Trading doesn't exactly fit into most of these definitions either.

So regardless of how highly developed one's trading strategies become, the act of trading will still violate the integrity of any belief that is in conflict with the act of trading or making money from trading. Eventually the unexpressed energy accumulating in these conflicting beliefs will build to the point where the trader will find himself behaving in a manner completely inconsistent with his trading rules or intent to make money. Often, he will even be aware that he is about to make a trading error, watch himself do it, and at the same time either feel powerless to stop himself or won't stop himself until he has lost enough money to compensate for the imbalance in his mental environment.

Now when these kinds of things happen, if we don't understand what is going on, it could cause us to feel inadequate in some way, if we judge ourselves harshly. Or we could be overcome by a sense of powerlessness and fear because we seemingly have no control over these unidentified internal forces that can exert so much control over our behavior. Without any awareness of the problem or effective tools for dealing with it, most people will attempt to build mental barriers to try and block these forces from manifesting in their behavior. Obviously, they don't work, which makes the whole situation even scarier. This is where the substance abuse comes into play. For example, a person who is an alcoholic knows he is a heavy drinker. At the most fundamental level a person drinks obsessively to separate his intellect from these inner forces he believes he has no control over. The more he blocks, the more the forces build and the more he has to drink to block. The more he drinks, the more everything deteriorates in his outer environment as a reflection of his inner environment. Eventually, the physical environment, his body, or both deteriorate so badly that he can no longer block the true state of his condition. He then acknowledges that "Yes, I am an alcoholic, and I need to change," meaning that "Yes, I need to address the issues in my life that caused me to start drinking in the first place."

The point of all this is: learning how to forget our painful memories or ignoring the existence of beliefs that don't support our intents does not in anyway reduce their potential to cause us to behave in certain ways. If we want to change unwanted behavior, we have to change the internal source of that behavior. Releasing ourselves from the limitations of our fears by healing our emotional wounds, changing the polarity of a belief, or decharging it altogether is something that we have to learn how to do by learning how to manage mental energy. If people knew of some way of managing their beliefs, memories, and associations, then the kind of painful cycles of forced awareness described earlier would never get started in the first place.

Thus far I have identified three forces in constant operation in our lives. First are all the external environmental forces that have the potential to act as a cause, where we, as individuals, experience an effect. Some of these outside environmental forces we will have some degree of understanding of and others we will not. Our degree of understanding and insight along with the extent to which we can act on what we know is directly proportional to the degree of satisfaction we will experience as we interact with the environment to fulfill our needs and achieve our goals. Implied within all the external forces—whether we understand them or not—are all the forces of change that automatically alter everything made of atoms and molecules consequently making what we do know—in terms of usefulness—obsolete at some point in time. For example, the chair you are sitting in to read this book is deteriorating over time. At some point it will no longer be able to support any weight, making your belief in its stability obsolete.

Second are the deep inner forces of curiosity and attraction that compel us to explore, learn about, and interact with the environment in seemingly predetermined ways. For example, there are things that we are naturally interested in learning about or learning how to do in relationship to all the other things that are available to learn about in the environment, but we have no natural interest—like someone who always wanted to be a musician, fire-fighter, actor, or doctor and pursues these vocations resulting in feelings of deep satisfaction about their lives. However, if the environment forces us into areas where there is no natural interest, we will experience an emptiness that can be very difficult to identify, only that it feels like something is missing in our lives. What each of us as individuals is naturally curious about and attracted to in the environment come from the deepest levels of our existence. They act as very powerful forces of self-expression, compelling us to create in the physical environment the object of our imagination or to pursue in the physical environment the object of our interests, often in direct conflict with outside environmental forces as well as inner mental forces in the form of what we have been taught to believe.

Third are the mental forces represented by our beliefs, memories, and associations. Even though beliefs, memories, and associations are mental forces, they are not the same as the forces of curiosity and attraction. Beliefs, memories, and associations exist exclusively as a result of the kinds of experiences we have with the physical environment. This is in contrast to the forces of curiosity and attraction that are in us before we are born and would seem to be either predetermined in a spiritual sense or genetically encoded. Some of our beliefs, memories, and associations will act as positive resources for interacting with the physical environment effectively and with some degree of satisfaction. Others, however, will have just the opposite effect. Many of our beliefs, memories, and associations are resources for failure, pain, and dissatisfaction because they lock us into only perceiving what we already know as well as cutting us off from our natural sense of curiosity. In other words, they specifically act as forces to prevent any further mental growth.

Now, since we have to interact with the physical environment to fulfill our needs and achieve our goals, the key to doing it to assure ourselves of experiencing greater levels of satisfaction is to acquire deeper levels of insight and understanding into the nature of these forces. That is, we need to stay in a constant state of learning. The only thing that really stops us from continuing to learn about the nature of these outside forces is the mental forces in the form of beliefs, memories, and associations that build up and as a result block our natural sense of curiosity, sometimes to the point of shutting down the learning process altogether.

There is some element of truth to the saying that you can't teach an old dog new tricks, except that it should really read "An old dog won't learn new tricks." It's not that it is impossible for someone regardless of their age to learn something new; the issue isn't ability. It is more a matter of resistance and refusal. That refusal comes from the sum total of everything we already believe, in essence saying, "Forget it—I already know everything I need to know." Of course, the consequences to such a stance toward the environment can be and often are devastating. And it invariably always takes some truly devastating event or a series of them before someone who has this kind of attitude will acknowledge that the reason for their plight is that they just refuse to allow any changes in their mental environment. Of course, this know-it-all attitude is very easy to recognize in someone else; the trick is learning how to recognize it ourselves, because it exists in all of us as a natural function of the ways in which beliefs, memories, and associations manage information.

To stay in a constant state of learning we need to learn how to adapt. To adapt we need to learn some specific mental techniques on how to consciously apply our thoughts to upgrade, modify, replace, or change the polarity (electrical charge) of various components in our mental environment that act as limiting or inhibiting forces on our perception and behavior, preventing us from gaining greater levels of correspondence with the physical environment. By consciously adapting, we are making ourselves available to learn how to fulfill our needs and achieve our goals in increasingly more satisfying ways. *Note:* Implied within fulfilling our needs and achieving our goals is the need to explore the object of our curiosities and attractions, which also get blocked by our beliefs, associations, and memories.

To adapt, we need to choose not to resist learning and change. This requires a willingness on our part to think outside of the limitations established by our beliefs, associations, and memories and a willingness to learn how to manage mental energy so we can release ourselves from the negative effects of our painful memories. When we learn how to change the polarity of a painful memory, it isn't painful any longer. When the memory is discharged or drained of the negatively charged energy, it will no longer have the potential to generate fear. Fear always limits the number of choices we perceive as available from the environment by the way it causes us to focus our attention on the object of our fear. The net effect is we end up creating for ourselves exactly what we are trying to avoid. It is important for you to note that, when we change the polarity of a memory, it doesn't actually change the structure of the memory. In other words, we don't forget the experience, so we can still use it as a part of our repertoire of what we know about the nature of the physical environment. When we change the quality of energy of a memory from negative to positive, we negate the memory's potential to generate fear, thereby allowing us to perceive all the other choices for experience available from the environment in the same moment.

Preferably this willingness to change will come from somewhere other than out of desperation. The idea is to learn how to recognize what we need to know long before the conditions deteriorate to the levels of desperation. To do this requires that we incorporate into our mental system three very fundamental assumptions that will help us to maintain a healthy relationship with the environment and generate the energy behind the willingness that we will need to start such a process, after which experiencing the benefits will act as the driving force behind our willingness.

The first assumption is that we haven't learned everything there is to know. And, as a result, there are always going to be unknown forces acting upon us until our understanding of everything outside of us evolves to the point where we have simultaneous awareness of everything going on in the environment. The implications here are that we need to be in a constant state of learning from the moment we are born to the moment we die because our intellect has not yet evolved to the point of simultaneous perception of all information that is available in any given moment. Until then, we are forced to pick and choose the information we experience based on what we have learned to believe.

The second assumption is that what we have learned to believe either by force—unwillingly thrust upon us, as an expression of the outside environment—or by choice—as an expression of inner forces that operate within us like our curiosity and attractions—may not be very useful with respect to fulfilling ourselves in some satisfying manner.

The third assumption is that what we have learned that is useful and works to our satisfaction is still subject to change because of the changing environmental conditions. In other words, what we may need to know to experience more satisfaction and happiness in our lives will often have to replace partially or invalidate completely what we have already learned. Refusing to change what we have already learned is virtually the same as saying that we already know everything there is to know and don't need to learn anything further. Of course, we could easily know if we didn't need to adapt because we would be in a perpetual state of satisfaction. Anything less than a feeling of satisfaction from our interaction with the environment is an indication that we need to learn something.

THE PERFECTION OF THE MOMENT

If you operate out of the foregoing assumptions, you will begin to recognize how every moment becomes a perfect indication of your state of development and what you need to do to improve yourself. For example, let's look at a hypothetical trader whose goal is to make money from his trading. He perceives what he believes to be an opportunity to do so and puts on a trade. However, he is operating out of a fear of being wrong. As a result, his fear will act on his perception of information to block from his awareness any evidence that would indicate that he is wrong. Remember that fear is a natural mechanism to warn us of threatening conditions so that we can avoid them. Now what is threatening about being wrong? In this case, as in most all cases, it is all the accumulated pain and humiliation inside of him from his past experiences. If the market—or anyone else for that matter—presents him with any information that conflicts with what he wants, his fear will cause him to distort it perceptually or he will angrily scream at the person who offered such information "Don't tell me that" so that he can avoid feeling the pain already inside of him from his past. In effect, his fears will create for him the very experience that he is trying to avoid because he is avoiding information that would indicate what the markets have to offer in relationship to what he wants or expects. If the market does move against him, he probably won't confront the evidence until the pain of doing so is less than the pain of not confronting it, meaning that his losses accumulate to the point where it is easier to admit he is wrong than to suffer any more losses.

The results of our efforts will be reflected in the environment as the sum total of who we are in any given moment, as it was for our trader in the foregoing example. A goal is an intent that we have projected out into the environment. It is a need to be fulfilled in some future moment. The need arises out of a recognition of some lack. Recognizing the need automatically focuses our attention to scan the environment for ways (paths) to fulfill that need. The environmental information we perceive (quality and depth of insight) will be a function of the number of distinctions we can make minus any information that gets blocked by any fears we are operating out of. How we express ourselves to fulfill the need will be function of (1) our perceptions, (2) the steps that we choose as a result of those perceptions, and (3) the skills we have developed minus any conflicting beliefs, memories, and associations, making each moment that we interact with the environment a perfect indication of what we know and how well we can act on what we know.

When we refuse to acknowledge or accept the perfection of each moment in our lives, we deny ourselves access to the information that we need to expand ourselves. Any skill that we need to learn to express ourselves more effectively has a true starting point. To find that true starting point requires our acceptance of each outcome as a reflection of the sum total of who we are so that we can first identify what skill needs to be learned and how we might go about the task of learning it. Without this true starting point, we will operate from a base of illusion.

Illusions result from beliefs that we know more than we do and can do more than we can. We erroneously assume the environment shares our perception of it or of ourselves and then we actively block any information to the contrary. Illusions are the difference between accepting each moment as a perfect indication of who we are so that we can identify what we need to learn to move forward and believing we are already perfect the way we are, in which case we need learn nothing. Certainly if any of us were in a perfect state of knowledge and abilities, then we would never need to complain about anything or make excuses, rationalizations, or justifications for why things didn't turn out as we planned.

Every "should have," "could have," "would have," or "if only" is an indication of the degree of illusion in which we are indulging ourselves. If we could have, we would have, meaning that at each moment we are doing the best we can when taking into account all the components—both conscious and subconscious—that affect what we perceive and do. Acknowledging and accepting this perfection will always give us our true starting point to indicate what we need to learn so that we can perceive the conditions differently or what resources we need to develop to respond differently.

If our hypothetical trader wants to develop into an effective and consistently successful trader, he will need to engage in some self-improvement. He will need to understand that the market is always right and that he can profit from that rightness if he doesn't impose a rigid mental structure on its behavior. He needs to release himself from his fear of being wrong so that he can observe the market's behavior from an objective perspective. Otherwise, his fear of being wrong will have the effect of making him wrong. He will also need to establish some definite trading rules to guide his own behavior and learn how to adhere to those rules. If he had been operating out of a definite set of trading rules he would have never let the loss accumulate sufficiently that his pain would take him out of the trade. If, however, he refuses to acknowledge and accept his current state of development by blaming the market for his losses or trying to convince himself that somehow he wasn't responsible for what he ended up with, then he would be indulging himself in illusion. He would be denying who he is and, in effect, cutting himself off from the information he needs to become who he wants to be.

We have to be willing to confront the truth about ourselves so that we can confront the truth outside of ourselves. The less illusion we indulge ourselves in, the more our perceptions of the outside environment will reflect the actual conditions, because we won't be blocking so much available information. By available information I mean information we are capable of perceiving. The less we block, the more we learn. The more we learn, the easier it is to anticipate how the outside environment will react or respond under any given set of conditions. Otherwise, we will not allow ourselves to perceive in the environment what we refuse to know about ourselves.

None of us likes to acknowledge what we perceive to be our weaknesses. Yet it is exactly what we need to do to grow beyond them. Otherwise, we keep building our lives on this base of illusion that requires so much energy, alcohol, or drugs to maintain that it eventually has to crumble, leading to these very painful forced awarenesses. Confronting the truth in the environment or the truth about ourselves is no more painful than are the forced awarenesses that result from these illusions. It's just more immediate. However, when we do confront what is inside of us, it is the first step in the process of breaking a cycle of dissatisfaction to turn it into an expansive cycle of success. What better form of goal achievement could there be than to confront conditions as they exist, identify what we need to learn to operate most effectively, and then go about the task of learning it, making our adjustments along the way?

ALL TRADERS GIVE THEMSELVES EXACTLY WHAT THEY DESERVE

Traders put on trades and then take them off when they choose. That decision-making process is the result of the sum total of all the mental components interacting with one another. If we were to inventory all these components, measure the energy they hold, and then balance the components that contribute to a positive sense of self-valuation against the components that contribute to a negative sense of self-valuation, what would be left is a net amount that we value ourselves. This net amount will correspond directly with how much money we give ourselves out of what is available in any given trade, in any day, month, or year, or by the same token how much of our money we give away.

I know that this can be a very difficult concept to accept. However, other than taking into account what we haven't learned yet in terms of insights and skills, how could it be any other way? We make up all our own rules when we trade. No one forces us in or out of the markets, unless a position is liquidated by a brokerage firm for lack of margin. In any given trade, there are a number of possibilities to take profits or cut losses. What we decide to do in each instance with respect to each possibility will be the result of our perceptions and all the internal components affecting those perceptions. What we actually end up doing will be the result of what we decide and our ability to execute our decisions, which again will be determined by a number of mental factors, all of which contribute to our sense of self-valuation.

Trading is an exercise in accumulating money. Once we have learned how to trade (perceive opportunity and execute our trades), who else or what else could be responsible for what we end up with? In fact, if traders were to chart their equity, it would reflect their internal conflicts and what they think of themselves on a day-to-day, month-to-month, or year-to-year basis. These charts would look very much like the typical bar or point and figure charts of the markets themselves, with support and resistance levels, consolidation zones, rallies, selloffs, and retracements. All these patterns would reflect the trader's state of mind, just as the markets themselves reflect the collective state of mind of all its participants.

Charts like these also can have the same predictive value as in the markets, if one learns what to look for. Some of the more sophisticated brokerage firms that manage large funds keep these kinds of charts on the CTAs that they employ to trade their money under management. They will switch the amount of equity available for each CTA to manage based on each individual's chart formations. In other words, once you build up some history it isn't too difficult to determine when someone is about to take a big hit because of the psychological forces building inside of him, just as the collective forces of the market build before a big move.

As individual traders if we want to give ourselves more and more money out of the markets, we have to learn how to value ourselves more and more so that we believe we deserve what we want or deserve what we get. Trading can result in the fast accumulation of windfall profits. To keep those profits, we have to have inner support. Most of the time, that support doesn't exist, and that accounts for all the rags to riches to rags stories that can be told in the trading world. Of course the first step in the process of valuing ourselves more is to accept our true starting point; that is, we have to take complete responsibility for what we end up with as being a reflection of what we need learn about the markets, about ourselves, or both. Ultimately, everything that we do contributes to or detracts from our sense of self-valuation. That is why it can fluctuate from day to day or moment to moment. The best way that I know of to add to our sense of valuation is to commit ourselves to the process of growth.

CHAPTER 13

Managing Mental Energy

What do I mean by "managing mental energy," you ask? There are many ways that we already manage mental energy but probably wouldn't think of it in such a way. For example, isn't it possible to take what starts out to be a slight emotional wound (like some minor insult) and intensify the emotional energy behind that wound to the point where we could end up in a state of emotional frenzy? How do we accomplish this? By our willingness to think about whatever caused us to feel insulted. Our thoughts can add energy to or detract energy from the wound, depending on what kind of thoughts we choose to think. If we think destructive thoughts, we will be adding negatively charged energy to intensify the wound. And it goes without saying that we can carry this to whatever extreme we choose and, furthermore, stop whenever we choose or whenever we are willing to. However, stopping does become more difficult in direct proportion to the amount of energy involved. Aren't we, in effect, managing or manipulating mental energy when we purposefully make ourselves more angry than when we started out by channeling negative thoughts through an experience?

By the same token, if we think positive thoughts, we will detract emotional energy from the wound. I am sure anyone reading this book has noticed that when a person wants to stay angry, he will refuse to listen to *anything* that might defuse his anger. When we refuse to listen to "the voice of reason" so to speak, we are making a choice not to manage mental energy. The only reason why an angry person has to shut out "the voice of reason" is because he knows the information has the potential to change the way he feels. He knows that if he changes his perspective—which will, in turn, change the way he feels—he will experience a different environment on the outside. If he isn't "willing" to change—regardless of what the benefits may be—he will refuse to use his thoughts in a way that would allow him to experience those benefits. These examples are just a few of the many ways in which we already manipulate our mental environment to suit our purposes based on our willingness to do so. Certainly, if it is possible to manage mental energy for destructive purposes, it must also be possible to manage it for constructive purposes. The key concepts here are willingness and purpose. The willingness is to consciously direct our thoughts toward a specific intent to change something on the inside that isn't useful.

Thoughts are a very powerful tool to effect changes in the mental environment. We can use them to shift, rearrange, add to, detract from, or change the polarity of various mental components. Thoughts are a form of energy, probably no different from electricity or light. They can act as a cause to produce some effect in the physical environment, as when we speak our thoughts, for example, as well as act as a cause to produce an effect in the mental environment. When we use our thoughts directed inward, we are basically using one form of energy as a tool to change the consistency and makeup of another form of energy, like using our thoughts to change a belief or release the negative energy out of a painful memory.

It is precisely because of the inherent power within thoughts that people are so protective of themselves with the kinds of information (others people's thoughts expressed physically) they will expose themselves to. Everyone instinctively knows that if we allow ourselves to think about something, the thoughts have the power to change the way things exist inside of us. And once things change on the inside, we know we will perceive and experience a different outside. If we don't want to disturb the current relationship be-tween inner and outer, we will consciously do whatever is necessary to make sure that we don't expose ourselves to anything that might threaten that relationship or think about anything in a way that would change the relationship. Change is the result of, first, a will-ingness to think.

Personally, I believe that if we weren't meant to keep on growing mentally (adding to who we are by transcending what we have al-ready learned) and furthermore if we weren't meant to direct that growth at a conscious level, then we would not have been given the ability to think, reason, and create. Implied within our ability to think, reason, and create is the inherent capability to learn our way out of the painful situations and dissatisfying life cycles in which we find ourselves. Painful life cycles begin with and are perpetuated by painful memories. So in essence what I am stating is that inherent within our ability to think and reason is the capability to heal our emotional wounds so that we can perceive what is available from the environment beyond our fears. Healing emotional wounds is some-thing that we have to learn how to do by learning how to manage mental energy. Learning how to forget our painful memories by making them subconscious does not in any way reduce their signifi-cance on our perception of environmental information, or their potential to cause us to behave in certain ways.

This is the gift of creativity that we were all born with. It is the capability to think beyond what our current beliefs, memories, and association would dictate as being true about the environment. *The capability to reason beyond our current set of limitations* (beliefs, pain-ful memories, and erroneous associations) *or use our imaginations creatively is the one compensating force that allows us to grow, improve, and evolve beyond the painful and destructive life cycles that we get caught in, both as individuals and as a culture.* However, there is something here that you may need to be mindful of: a capability to do something is not necessarily an ability to do something. Before a capability becomes an ability, it has to be cultivated into a skill. For example, we can use our imaginations to visualize and then project into the environment the fulfillment of some need or goal in some future moment. But that doesn't mean we are using our imagina-tions creatively. We may just be using our imaginations to project what is already in our memories or what we already believe. The same is true for our thoughts. Most of the time, they will originate out of our current set of beliefs and memories, so that what we will be thinking will correspond with the status quo. To create a more satisfying future for ourselves, we need to be able to imagine this future and project it out into the environment as some future moment. There is a direct correlation between what we project and what is already inside of us, unless of course, we are imagining something beyond what we already know.

The only real limitations that exist with respect to thought are those rules that were either taught to us or the ones we made up for ourselves. We are not in any way restricted to just thinking about what we already believe is true or what we have already experienced. We are free to roam anywhere in our thoughts to explore any number of possibilities and choose to act on one of them, regardless of whether it is inside or outside of the current set of rules from which we operate, even to the point of using our thoughts to change any rules that we may have that says we can't. If we weren't meant to direct our own changes by thinking about how we might learn how to lead happier and more satisfying lives, then thinking, reasoning, and creativity wouldn't exist.

To experience the same kind of painful conditions over and over again, in an environment that is in constant motion, implies that we don't perceive any other choices as being available that would result in more satisfying outcomes. What we perceive is directly connected to what we already know. To perceive other choices, other than the ones our beliefs, memories, and associations lock us into, we have to know something we haven't learned yet. So, learning our way out of a situation that is perpetually dissatisfying requires that we be open to thinking beyond what we already know. The environment will always offer us an opportunity for some degree of love, harmony, happiness, and success or some degree of despair, disappointment, anger, hate, and betrayal. What we end up with from each of these moments has to be a reflection of what is inside of us because the environment does not interpret the information it has to offer in any given moment. That process happens exclusively in each one of us. Remember the free money example in Chapter 10? The reality of pleasure existed right along with the reality of indifference or fear. The man was there to give money to anyone who wanted. How each person interpreted the data determined what reality they experienced.

Creativity is synonymous with growth and change. Doesn't the word "create" imply bringing into existence something that did not previously exist? If it already existed, then it would have already been created. To use our imaginations creatively, we must to be willing to think outside of what we already know to be true or possible. For those of you who are not that familiar with various forms of creative thinking, you would be surprised how just the willingness to question the usefulness of something inside of us will bring forth an avalanche of inspiring alternatives. Otherwise, our memories and beliefs will cause us to think of the future in ways that directly correspond with our past, thus having the effect of locking us into the same recurring experiences. The names and places may change but the situations and circumstances and conditions always remain the same because we aren't changing our mental framework to perceive anything different.

"Necessity is the mother of invention!" In other words, the need to create some new machine, device, or process to save time, save money, or make money isn't any different from the need to "create a new you" to experience success and a more satisfying life. The need will act as a force behind our thoughts to think beyond our current barriers so that we can expand. The barriers that act as a resisting force preventing us from expanding consist of many of our beliefs and all our painful memories. So we need a force to counteract and penetrate those barriers. That force is our thoughts and our willingness to use them in creative ways.

All our lives would become a lot easier to live and potentially more satisfying if we operated out of the belief that we are in a state of imperfect knowledge, evolving toward something that we haven't become yet. Everything is evolving into something that it isn't yet. It may not seem like it at times, but each moment of each day, we change into someone who was not the person we were a moment ago. At the physical level new cells are born and old cells die. At the mental level each moment that passes we experience something. Each experience adds to the inner environment in the form of a memory or belief. Each memory and belief builds a self-concept that acts as a force on how we interact with the environment. Then as we interact with the environment, we change it in some way, creating a new environment for us to discover and experience. Everything that exists is evolving, because everything that exists is in motion, and motion creates change. Even the grandest mountain will eventually wear away into small rocks, which will themselves turn into sand and then dust.

However, the main point here is that implied within this concept of evolution (where we are in a state of imperfect knowledge) is the view that mistakes don't exist. Mistakes just point the way to something that we haven't learned yet and obviously need to know. What exactly is a mistake anyway? We certainly weren't born with a concept or definition of what a mistake is. If left alone, all children will naturally keep on interacting with the environment to satisfy their own inner needs to learn and grow until they start to learn that what they are doing isn't quite up to the standards set by the people who are watching them. And all children just loved to be watched.

The criteria that we use for how we define a mistake is something that we had to learn from someone. In other words, our parents and teachers passed their definitions on to us. These definitions would represent the mental framework for their unresolved painful experiences and what they themselves haven't learned about as being available from the environment beyond their pain. In other words, we pass on our ignorance, as well as our wisdom, without knowing at the time the difference between the two. And what was passed on that was dysfunctional will be regarded as the truth just the same as the wisdom.

When we as adults instill in our children our rigid definitions of what constitutes a mistake (thinking that what we are going to do is save them), all we are really doing is perpetuating our pain in the next generation. A mistake isn't resolved until we evolve in our understanding to the point where we can garner the insight that is available from the experience. When that point is reached, what we experienced is no longer a mistake or painful because of what we have learned. However, until that point is reached, if ever, we will feel compelled to save others from the painful lessons of our mistakes, even to the point of beating it into them—for their own good, of course. By using pain, either emotional or physical as a means to save others from our mistakes, in effect what we are really doing is creating a cycle of fear. We ensure that our limited level of understanding and insight will be maintained in them because fear is a contracting force that stifles the learning process. In a very real way, we inflict the pain of our unresolved mistakes on our children just as our parents inflicted the pain of their unresolved mistakes on us. And it goes on generation after generation until someone decides to use their creative powers to break the cycle.

To operate out of this belief in evolution so that we can naturally learn from the choices that we make, we have to first change our definitions of what constitutes a mistake. It is precisely these kinds of beliefs that act as mental blocks to perceive a more satisfying way of living. Mistakes are virtually synonymous with pain. We can find any number of ways to avoid acknowledging a mistake so we don't have to confront the pain, and in the process we cut ourselves off from what we need to know to grow, expand, and improve our lives. Even when we make a mistake where we supposedly knew better, if we really knew better, then we wouldn't have made the choices that we did that resulted in an outcome we define as a mistake. So we can assume that there is something inside of us that conflicts with our "better judgment" that has more power to influence our behavior.

It isn't any less possible to change our definition of what constitutes a mistake than it is to intensify the emotional energy behind an insult as in the example. To change these definitions requires learning some techniques in mental energy management to de-energize or draw the negatively charged energy out of them. By doing so we will allow ourselves to learn from all our experiences instead of hiding from them, feeling pain, or punishing ourselves in some way. Without the effects of these self-defeating definitions of mistakes, it is much easier to objectively monitor our progress toward the fulfillment of some goal. If we find our behavior inconsistent with the steps to achieving our goals it would tell us that our beliefs are not in harmony with those steps or the goal itself or that we don't have the appropriate resources. In any case, it is much easier to identify what we need to learn to accomplish our objective.

THE BENEFITS OF LEARNING
HOW TO MANAGE MENTAL ENERGY

Increased Sense of Security and Confidence

You will develop a sense of security and confidence knowing that you can confront conditions as they exist, identify what you need to learn to operate most effectively, and learn it. What better way to develop a sense of security than by learning how to develop the ability to adapt to the prevailing conditions to fulfill your needs satisfactorily.

In the mental environment the memories of our experiences don't change over time, but the physical environment where our goals are fulfilled does. It is constantly moving forward, offering us new conditions, which, in turn, offer us different possibilities and opportunities, if we are open to being able to perceive them. What better form of goal achievement than to be able to change our mental perspective "at will" to be able to perceive these new conditions and use our imaginations creatively to determine the most appropriate set of steps to fulfill our needs or achieve our goals, even if we have never actually taken those steps before?

For a truly successful trader, this form of thinking is essential. The possibilities of the type of movement the markets can display are almost endless because of the diverse number of forces affecting it. All of us have this tendency to mentally lock ourselves into only a very limited number of those ways. And when the market doesn't conform to our preconceived mental image, we make up the difference with distortions and illusions and suffer the consequences later. Trading doesn't have to be painful and devoid of fun. We make it that way for ourselves because of our mental inflexibility and inability to adapt.

Increased Levels of Satisfaction

As long as we are alive, we will have needs, and as long as we have needs, we are not whole the way we are. Our needs compel us to interact with the environment to achieve this state of wholeness. Growing into this state of wholeness requires that we keep on learning. To keep on learning we need to adapt. Learning is a primary function of our existence. When we fulfill this function, we are rewarded with feelings of happiness, well-being and satisfaction, all of which are by-products of the quality of our experiences with the outer environment and a function of how much we have learned.

The antithesis of learning is resistance. When we resist what is being offered by the environment in the way of lessons, learning, and change we experience stress. Stress is the opposite of the sense of well-being, happiness, and excitement that we feel when we are learning. If we refuse to adapt, we shut down the learning process. The quality of our experiences deteriorates because our relationship with the outer environment deteriorates. The outer environment keeps on changing, while we remain unchanged, resulting in less of a correspondence between what is out there and what we know. Ultimately, we end up punishing ourselves for our resistance to adapt because what we experience is pain, disappointment, stress, anxiety, and dissatisfaction, which are all by-products of our lack of insight, understanding, and what we won't allow ourselves to do because of fear.

Increased Intuition

As you gain in your confidence to change the inside to experience a different outside, you will also increase your ability to confront difficult issues that all of us would have a tendency to avoid. Instead of confronting, we learn a number of avoidance techniques like alcohol, drugs, distortions, rationalizations, or even wishing and hoping, all of which can result in painful forced awarenesses. We eventually have to confront these issues anyway because they rarely if ever (just) go away. The longer we wait, the worse the conditions usually get, making it increasingly more difficult to resolve.

However, there is another less obvious problem with avoidance, especially with respect to wishing and hoping. A true intuitive impulse—a deeper level of knowledge and wisdom that will indicate the next most appropriate step to take—that will always be in our best interests feels very much like wishing and hoping. In other words, it is very difficult to distinguish between the two, making it very easy to mix them up, which is one of the reasons why we find it so difficult to trust our intuition. The way you can know for sure that you are getting a true intuitive impulse is to clear out of your mental environment anything that would cause you to wish and hope that something will happen instead of confronting the issue head on to find out what needs to be done. You can wish and hope that the market will come back, or you can cut your loss and make yourself ready to take the next opportunity. To be able to cut your loss and be ready to take the next opportunity requires that you change anything in your mental environment that would cause you to avoid confrontation and consequently wish and hope. The less cause you have for wishing and hoping that something will happen, the more you will know that when you get that certain feeling, it is a true intuitive impulse, and the more confidence you will have to follow it. Intuition will always guide you in the most appropriate way to fulfill your needs.

Just so there is no misunderstanding here, I am not stating that there is anything inherently wrong with wishing and hoping. There are some ways in which wishing and hoping can be very useful. As traders, however, we cannot afford the luxury of wishing and hoping because it puts us in a passive relationship with the markets. When we wish and hope, we are shifting responsibility on to the markets for making something happen instead of confronting the conditions and doing something about it ourselves. If we find ourselves wishing and hoping, it is an excellent indication that we don't know what is going on and as a result need to get out of the markets until we do.

Wisdom

When we step through our fears to break some cycle of frustration and dissatisfaction or change the polarity of a painful memory to break a cycle of pain, we gain in wisdom because we learn all sides of an issue. Wisdom is not afraid, angry, intolerant, or prejudiced because there is a deep level of understanding, confidence, and trust, all coming from having experienced the full range of possibilities from extreme negative to increasingly greater degrees of positive. If we have experienced only the negative side of a certain type of experience, we feel fear. If we have experienced only the positive (never having had a painful experience in certain area), we won't have that particular fear, but we do develop an intolerance or even a disdain for anyone who has had a negative experience.

This intolerance stems from our own underlying fear of vulnerability. For instance, it is clear that the negative exists in the environment as a possibility, but since it has never happened to us, we either don't understand "their fear" or don't want to confront any information that would indicate the same possibilities for a painful experience also exist for us. Anyone who has truly transcended a fear doesn't look down upon those who haven't because they don't have anything to fear. When we step through some fear to experience other possibilities, not only do we give ourselves more choices, we also gain in wisdom. Wisdom is the by-product that results when we retain a distinction about the nature of the environment without the negative energy or fear associated with that distinction. Wisdom is ultimately the silver lining in every dark cloud.

However, to gain this wisdom we have to actively change our negatives into positives, because if we are offered a positive experience in an area where we have only experienced the negative, we wouldn't believe it. Actually we couldn't believe it, because we wouldn't have the mental framework to accept it for what it is. The environment will be as we perceive it, and the way we perceive information and events is controlled by the energy already inside of us, unless it is a first-time experience. When we don't actively work at turning our negatives into positives, we just stay angry and afraid. It's our choice. We were all given the gift of creativity and the free will to think any way in which we choose, and we can use our thoughts to change the quality of our lives, if we want to.

CHAPTER 14

Techniques for Effecting Change

This chapter offers various techniques for effecting change. Also included are various exercises to implement these changes.

DIRECTING A CONSCIOUS SHIFT IN BELIEF SYSTEMS

The conscious mind (that part of us that is aware of the our surroundings and what we are thinking at any given moment) can generate thoughts outside of the framework of our beliefs or belief systems. In other words, we can ask questions about the validity or usefulness of any belief and purposefully direct our attention to any area where we might discover something more useful or better suited to the conditions. Any new knowledge comes from those who question the status quo and have a willingness to go beyond and a willingness to accept the next answer.

I know this is probably going to sound overly simplistic to most readers, and it is also something everybody already knows, but not everybody knows it within the context of changing beliefs: *The wanting to is the how.* To identify or change anything in the mental environment requires that you *want to,* because to want something you have to think about it, and when we think about something, we are generating thought energy. This is the same energy that our beliefs, memories, and associations are composed of, and, as such, thoughts have the power to change, reorganize, add to, detract from, or change the polarity of anything in the mental environment. In essence you can use our thoughts to create a new identity because we *want to.*

Each choice we make on a conscious level, even just to choose to redirect our thoughts from an inappropriate belief (relative to our needs now), will start to make a neurological change in the electrical circuitry of our brain. If you go as far as to make a choice that is inconsistent with a belief you want to discharge and then act out of that belief, it will eventually lose its power and consequently lose its potential to affect our behavior.

It is important for you to understand that beliefs cannot be destroyed; once we have formed one, it will be with us for the rest of our lives. However, we can draw all the energy out of them. For example, a pile of wood set on fire will release the energy of the wood into the atmosphere as heat. The wood will be transformed into ashes. The ashes do not have the potential to produce any heat and, thus, will have little if any effect on the environment. Yet the ashes still exist. De-energized beliefs work the same way. They will always exist but no longer have any effect on our perception of information or our behavior. Many of us once believed in the tooth fairy and the bogeyman in the closet. Eventually these beliefs just naturally collapsed as we learned more about the nature of the environment. Up to that point, however, they definitely had an effect on our perception of information and behavior. Now, we can say I remember when I used to believe that. To remember that we used to believe something means that the belief still exists; it just no longer has any power in our mental system.

Each belief you identify will form a comfort zone. The boundaries of this comfort zone are set by the limitations inherent within any belief that make up the zone. All definitions set boundary lines and make distinctions. Each belief is our truth about reality. Beliefs define not only our environment, but also who we are in relation to that environment. These definitions establish the amount of tolerance for awareness that we have for what exists in both the internal and external environment. For example, do you have a belief that would allow for the possibility of the market doing anything at any given moment? If not, what do you believe can't happen? If what you believe can't happen did happen, how long would it take you to be able to recognize it, if at all? Notice the boundary lines in awareness created by the structure of the belief.

There is one thing you should keep in mind as you learn to change your beliefs to be more reflective of your intents and goals. With all change there is struggle. Volcanos, childbirth, social revolution, wind, rain, and waves are all examples of the violent nature of the forces of change. That is why so many people find it difficult to be creative. We are attracted and compelled toward creativity, on the one hand, because it is an inherent part of our nature. However, on the other hand, we don't want to confront the conflict and ensuing struggle between the old and the new. It is essentially the same when you change a belief. There will be some conflict or some degree of uncomfortableness as you move from one set of beliefs to another. However, the uncomfortableness does pass, and just like anything else, the more you do it, the easier it gets, until it becomes a learned skill that you can use just like any other that is a part of who you are.

EXERCISE TO IDENTIFY CONFLICTING BELIEFS

Set a timer for 10 minutes.

Write a series of statements that begin with "I am."

Write as fast as you can and let every thought come to your conscious attention. It is extremely important that you do not censor any statements, especially the contradictory ones.

At the end of the 10 minutes, look at the list and cross out everything that is a fact. For example, you would cross out statements such as I am a man/woman, I am blue-eyed, I am brown-haired.

All the statements that remain are the beliefs you are looking for. The beliefs that contradict each other are of particular importance. Contradictory beliefs cancel your energy because you have a built-in mental conflict between the validity of one belief expressing itself only at the direct expense of another belief.

What are some examples of conflicting or contradictory beliefs?

I have to win./I may be undeserving.

I am a winner./I am a loser.

I am successful./I've missed my chance to be successful.

I deserve more./I am guilty.

I am a perfectionist./I believe humans are inherently imperfect.

I am trusting./I am untrustworthy or people are generally untrustworthy.

I believe there is no middle ground of satisfaction between winning and failure./I am pleased with myself and my progress.

I am honest./I am dishonest or people are generally dishonest.

I believe working is the honest way of making money./I believe trading is easy money, not work.

Asking Yourself Questions

Here are some questions you can ask yourself that will help you to identify some beliefs that may argue against your giving yourself more money.

What do you believe about guilt?

How do you know when to feel guilty?

Under what conditions would you not feel guilty, even if someone else wanted you to?

Is it possible to transfer those same standards to areas where you would feel guilty?

What would stop you?

Who or what out of your past says it is wrong and you can't do that?

Is their assessment of reality any more valid than yours? If so, why?

Do you find these beliefs useful? If so, in what ways?

Do you find them limiting? If so, in what ways?

If you could identify and change the experience that created the belief, how would you change it?

What would stop you from changing it?

For the following questions you can substitute the words "is true" for the words "do you believe."

What do you believe about competition?

What do you believe about taking money from other people as a result of your superior trading skills?

What do you believe about losses?

What do you believe about other people's opinions?

When are they valid? When aren't they valid?

What do you believe about being wrong?

By answering these questions, you will begin to gain a sense of your own particular behavior and the range of choices you allow for yourself, or do not allow for yourself, as a result of your beliefs.

Sometimes it is easier to identify a belief by trying to notice what you specifically believe is not true. You could also look at your beliefs as if they belonged to someone else. If they did belong to someone else, think of an experience in which this other person responded to certain life situations in very typical ways (because of your beliefs). Then think of ways he or she could respond if he or she had different beliefs.

When you discover some beliefs that aren't particularly useful or are inconsistent with your goals, then use an affirmation or collapsing technique to discharge the energy out of it.

WRITING AS A TECHNIQUE TO
EFFECT CHANGE

Every movement we make alters the physical landscape in some way. The more dramatic or expressive our movements, the greater the alterations. By the same token, every thought alters the mental landscape in some way. The more expressive our thoughts, in other words, the more energy we generate in our willingness to think, the greater the potential to effect some change. The change comes from what we are willing to think. Wanting to direct your conscious thought process toward a specific intent is what effects this change. I have found writing is one of the most powerful tools available to focus my thinking and effect some change I desire.

When we write it is a physicalized version of what is going on inside of our mental environment. Your willingness to write about certain issues directs your attention and gives the rest of the parts of your mental environment instructions. What flows up or out of your consciousness is what is there. Once you find out what is there, you can then direct any changes by writing back instructions into the mental environment. This can be a very powerful technique, depending on how much power you put into it.

If I were to do a schematic of the process it would look something like this:

Consciousness ⟶ to ⟶ Mental environment (instructions for certain information).

The information flows to consciousness (maybe not right away). Consciousness physicalizes the information by writing it; this makes it real and tangible. Consciousness becomes aware of the information (self-discovery). Consciousness makes the connections between the nature of the information and the life conditions one has been experiencing. Consciousness assesses the current structure of the mental environment for its usefulness. Consciousness wants to create new conditions. Consciousness asks, "What beliefs do I need as resources to be more effective or create the conditions I desire?" This is the beauty and essence of the creative process—to ask yourself a question and wait for the answer to pop into your consciousness or allow yourself to be directed to the answer. Consciousness will know when it has found the most appropriate answer because it will ring true in your mind or you will feel the truth of it in your body. Consciousness then formulates these new awarenesses into instructions for change. Then consciousness writes these changes back into the mental environment, giving yourself instructions to accept these new awarenesses as truth. The act of writing forces us to focus our thoughts in a manner that is consistent with what we want to create, and those thoughts alter the mental landscape.

AN EXERCISE TO DEVELOP
SELF-DISCIPLINE

Self-discipline is a word used to describe a process of learning how to take conscious control of your actions. It is not a personality trait or something you are born with. It is a specific thought methodology, a mental resource, that allows you to change a belief or belief system when it is in conflict with some goal or objective. Self-discipline is a more direct method of effecting some change because you would be purposefully acting in a manner that is in direct conflict with whatever you want to change.

So I would define self-discipline as willfully behaving outside of the boundaries of some belief (dealing with the emotional discomfort your actions will produce) to accomplish a certain goal or task that is inconsistent with that belief. If you work outside of that belief long enough, it will eventually de-energize. The rate at which the under-lying belief will de-energize is really not a function of time but rather intensity. In other words, the greater the intensity of our willingness and resolve, the faster the conflicting belief will lose its power.

For example, let's say you want to quit smoking or lose weight. These are conscious goals. Your beliefs (at least some of them) will be in conflict with these goals. The belief system supporting the smoker definition will probably have a great deal of power in your mental system. You can gauge the power of these beliefs or any beliefs by paying attention to how much discomfort and resistance you feel when you attempt to act (a conscious decision) in a way that is inconsistent with them. It is very difficult thing to do. It's as if beliefs take on a life of their own and demand expression both in our thoughts and behavior.

You can change these or any other definitions of yourself. However, you must first identify them and then determine how useful they are in helping you get what you want. You could ask yourself, "Is this belief a resource or obstacle to the successful fulfillment of my goal?" One way you can change these definitions is to build a mental resource for the sole purpose of changing beliefs that are not useful. I am going to call this mental resource "self-discipline."

Here is an exercise that will help you learn specifically how to develop and use self-discipline in your life. The purpose of this exercise is to help you learn how to use your mind in different ways. You'll be training your mind to stay positively focused on what you consciously want. You will also learn how to gauge internal resistance from belief systems, and how to build mental resources for taking conscious control of your life.

1. Make a list of several things you dislike doing, feel you can't do, or would like to stop doing or some things you have never done before and think you might enjoy. You could start a jogging or exercise program or take out the garbage on a regular basis, for example.

2. Once you have your list, look it over and pick a task that has a very low priority in your life or one of the least important items.

3. Next, tell yourself in the most positive way that doing this new task you have consciously decided upon is something you now want in your life. Don't say you are going to try and do it. A commitment to try to fulfill a goal is not strong enough.

4. Set up a rigid schedule for yourself to accomplish this new goal.

5. With each attempt to adhere to your schedule, keep track of your thought process or stream of thoughts by writing them down. At this point you might be saying to yourself, "How do I keep track of my thought process?"

In the physical environment we are constantly being bombarded with all sorts of information competing for our attention. We are aware of many things going on around us simultaneously. In effect our consciousness is split in many different directions at the same moment. Use a part of your consciousness to pay attention to what is going on inside of your head. You will be using a part of yourself to monitor your stream of thoughts as if they didn't belong to you. If you can temporarily act as if you were monitoring someone else's stream of thoughts, it may be much easier to gather the information you need to make this exercise meaningful.

6. As you attempt to adhere to your schedule, do you find yourself experiencing resistance, excuses, or rationalizations? If so, notice how these thoughts divert your conscious attention away from your goal. This is a classic example of a conflict between the conscious goal you have set for yourself and your belief system that doesn't have a belief or definition that corresponds with what you consciously want to do.

7. At this point you need to redirect your attention to the task you have chosen for yourself. What is most important is that you understand the necessity of directing as much energy toward the fulfillment of your goal as possible. You will have to generate more power toward keeping your attention focused on your goal than the amount of energy being directed through the beliefs that distract your attention away from your goal.

However, there is one aspect to this exercise I must caution you about. Redirecting your attention away from what distracts you to what you consciously want, does not mean that you suppress or deny what may be distracting you. Acceptance and acknowledgment of what exists within you will allow you to work with it. Suppression and denial require a lot of energy; this has the effect of supporting the beliefs you are trying to suppress. Be gentle with yourself.

Each time you set out to accomplish your task, and do so, you create a resource that helps you do it again. Each success will draw some energy away from the beliefs that acted as obstacles. With each success you will also be allocating energy to the new definition of yourself. This new definition allows you to start the task each time with greater and greater ease until the definition becomes a fundamental part of your mental system. When that happens, your actions concerning this task will seem automatic.

The most important aspect of this exercise is the experience you gain in understanding the process of changing beliefs. Each time you set out to change a belief or set of beliefs, you'll gain a resource that enables you to do it again. Each success you experience will help develop another set of beliefs that allow you to change more beliefs if and when it suits your purposes. You will establish a new definition of yourself that says: "I believe I can identify and change any belief about myself that may be in conflict with my conscious goals."

For this exercise to be effective, you must keep a few rules in mind.

First, start the exercise with a task or goal that is truly insignificant and has little meaning in your life. The objective of the exercise is learning how to manipulate your inner environment consciously and direct your conscious focus of attention. The goal you decide upon as the object of the exercise should not have a lot of value attached to the outcome. If it does, that would be an indication you may be taking on some very powerful and entrenched belief systems. This is something you definitely want to avoid until you have developed the necessary skills and resources.

Then, recognize that from the moment we are born, we are taught how to manipulate the outer physical environment; however, you may not have the resources to be even minimally effective at manipulating the mental environment. As a result, it is extremely important that you do not judge your ability to execute the schedule you set up according to the standards of performance you expect of yourself in the physical environment. If you expect too much and judge your ability harshly, it will only negate your efforts and set up a fear and inadequacy cycle. The less you expect of yourself, the faster you will progress. An expectation can easily become a demand that it be fulfilled. Demands usually generate a certain amount of fear that the demands will not be met. When you are working in the inner environment, fear will always negate your positive efforts unless your intent is to identify the source of your fear.

Finally, not having any expectations from your efforts to carry out your plan will also have the secondary benefit of helping you to learn to accept whatever you accomplish as being all right. Any step, no matter how small, is a step. Just deciding you want to do this exercise is significant, even if you don't follow through with it right away. You may come back to it some day when you have more of a "sense" of the power you will acquire from the ability to manipulate your inner environment consciously to be consistent with your goals. So, to keep yourself from having any expectation about how well you should do at this or any other exercise I offer you, I suggest you consider yourself an infant in a brand new environment. You will have to learn how to stand up before you can begin to walk or run.

SELF-HYPNOSIS

Self-hypnosis is a relaxation technique that allows one to bypass the reasoning process of the conscious mind to make it easier to accept some message. So it is an excellent technique for establishing new beliefs or collapsing old beliefs. For those of you who are interested, I have a self-hypnosis tape specifically designed to make it easier to learn how to cut your losses, reverse yourself, trust your intuition, and value yourself more. For more information, you can contact me at Trading Behavior Dynamics, Inc., in Chicago or through the publisher.

POSITIVE AFFIRMATIONS

When you are in a trade and start to experience anxiety about what is happening in the market, you will likely take those anxious thoughts and start running them through a negative loop—like thinking about money instead of the structure of the market or what the market is doing to you. Eventually you will run enough thought energy through your consciousness that it will cause you to act in a way that is not in your best interests. A positive affirmation will work the same way. Formulate a positive affirmation of some trait or characteristic of the way in which you want to be. For example, you may want to become a more patient person and wait for the market to give the signals to act. With an affirmation like "I am becoming a more patient person every day," you will eventually become that person. In other words we will behave in a manner that is consistent with the affirmation, if we run enough thought energy through that affirmation. Eventually, the affirmation becomes a belief with enough energy to affect our behavior.

The following are affirmations that, once turned into beliefs, will be very effective resources in helping you to work in your inner environment.

1. All beliefs are about reality, and are not necessarily predominate characteristics of reality. I will examine and question my beliefs in relationship to their usefulness in achieving my goals.

2. I believe in the power of my conscious mind to make available to me all the information I need to know.

3. I have the power to change any belief in a way that would make it more useful in achieving my goals of happiness, harmony, financial wealth, and being more productive.

4. I believe I am free to change the way I feel about any past experience.

5. I believe I have the ability to examine the contents of my mind.

6. I trust that all my beliefs about the way I trade will become known to me.

7. I place no particular importance on these beliefs about trading other than the fact that they exist.

8. I have chosen these beliefs at certain points in my life and accepted them as true at the time. As I examine them, I realize that they may not be particularly useful or true for me now. I accept this and I feel free to change all those beliefs that are inconsistent with my current goals.

9. My first and immediate goal is to identify all my beliefs that may be in conflict with my long-term objectives of _____ _____.

10. I trust myself to become consciously aware of these beliefs in many different ways. Once I become aware of these beliefs, I can just as easily let them go to make space for new beliefs that are more consistent with my current goals.

11. I believe that changing and expanding my awareness and comfort zones are a necessary aspect of my growth and

survival, and I welcome these opportunities to identify old beliefs and consequently grow and expand.

12. I feel an intense desire to succeed and achieve my goal of _____. Consequently I have an intense desire to clear my inner path of any resistance or obstructions that stand in the way of the fulfillment of my goal.

PART IV

How to Become a Disciplined Trader

CHAPTER 15

The Psychology of
Price Movement

My objective for this chapter is to break down and analyze the dynamics and psychology of price movement, first, at its most fundamental level, that of the individual trader; then I will broaden the explanation by examining the behavior of traders collectively as a group. I want to demonstrate that, if you understand the psychological forces inherent within traders' actions, you can easily determine what they believe about the future by just observing what they do. Once you know what traders believe about the future, it's not that difficult to anticipate what they are likely to do next, under certain circumstances and conditions.

What is really important about this insight is that it will help you to understand the distinctions between wishful thinking and the actual potential that exists for the market to move in any given direction. You will be learning to let the market tell you what to do by understanding the forces behind its behavior and then learning to differentiate between pure, uncontaminated market information and how that information is distorted once it starts doing something to you.

The most fundamental component of the markets is traders. Keep in mind that traders are the only force that can act on prices to make them move. Everything else is secondary. What makes a market? Two traders willing to trade, one wanting to buy and one wanting to sell, who agree on a price and then make a trade.

What does the last posted price represent? The last posted price is what someone was willing to pay and what someone was willing to sell for at the moment the two traders agreed on the trade. It reflects an agreement in present value between those traders acting at that price.

What is the bid? A trader announcing the price at which he is willing to buy. What is the offer? A trader announcing the price at which he is willing to sell. How do traders make money? There are only two ways to play this game to make money. To buy at a price you believe is low relative to where you can sell it back at some future point in time. Or to sell at a price you believe is high relative to where you can buy it back at some future point in time.

Now, let's take a look inside the pit to see what has to happen for prices to move off equilibrium and how this will tell us what traders believe.

98-18   The offer, sellers attempting to sell high.

98-17   Equilibrium, the last price.

98-16   The bid, buyers attempting to buy low.

Since the only object to trading is to make money we can assume that a trader will not knowingly enter into a trade believing he is going to lose. And for a trade to exist requires two traders who agree on a price. However, from the moment two traders agree to the trade, they are both subjecting themselves to market risk. In other words, the next tick is going to make one of them a winner and the other a loser. Since we know that both traders want to win and neither trader wants to lose, we can assume that both traders have completely opposite beliefs about the future value of the contract. So for two traders to agree on a price and make a trade, they have to have diametrically opposing beliefs about the future. The buyer believes he is buying low relative to where he can sell back at some point in the future, and the seller believes he is selling high relative to where he can buy back at some point in the future.

If the next tick is going to make one of them a winner and one a loser, we can assume that neither one of them believes he is going to be that loser. If the seller believed the next tick was going to be up, why wouldn't he have waited to sell it higher? The same is true for the buyer. That is the object of the game and the only way to make money. Basically what we have is a situation where two opposing forces are clashing; both believe they are right about the future, and only one side can profit at the direct expense of the other.

If the last price of a bond future was 99-14, what has to happen for the price to move to 99-15? Very simply, some trader has to be willing to bid and pay higher than the last price. This means that relative to the last posted price, he has to be willing to do the opposite of buying low. Any trader or group of traders willing to buy high or sell low relative to the last posted price is very significant for several reasons.

First, a trader willing to buy high or sell low instead of buy low or sell high has to have a stronger conviction in his belief in the future value, even if his conviction is out of panic. Second, he is making the last price a bottom. Third, he is aggressively taking the initiative and is making losers out of everyone who sold at the last price and deepened the losses of those who sold lower. Fourth, he is creating price movement that can possibly gather momentum if other traders perceive the new price as low relative to the future. This will also be true for the trader who is paying up to liquidate a position. On the other hand, the seller on the other side of his trade is being lured into the market by the attractiveness of the high price at which he can sell. He believes he is getting the edge. He is in fact selling high, but he is not creating movement or much of a possibility for momentum in his direction. He is picking a top and waiting for something to happen, hoping it won't go any higher.

Now, what do the actions of the two traders represent about the market in its collective form? First, this trade tells us that nobody had a strong enough belief in the future value to risk selling it to him at the last price or lower. Second, nobody was aggressive enough to want to enter the market short or liquidate an existing long position by offering to sell it at the last price or lower. A consummated trade at the next higher level creates a new equilibrium. This new equilibrium makes winners out of all the buyers at the last level and losers of all the sellers at the last level.

All of the losers at the last price level or lower would have to maintain a belief in the future value to stay in their position or demonstrate a conviction in this future value by adding on to their positions. This is because each new level the price is bid up makes it that much more attractive to them. If they believed it was high at lower levels, at each higher level, it's even a better trade. However, at the same time, each move the market makes against their position invalidates the sellers' expectation of future value. Each move clearly demonstrates that the sellers are passive, that the buyers are the aggressors, and that the buyers have a greater potential to move the market in their direction.

The fact that buyers are aggressively bidding up the price and paying more and more again tells the observer something. It tells him there aren't enough sellers to meet the buyers' demand for a trade at each new price level. If there is a limited supply of sellers, those traders wanting to buy will have to compete among one another for the limited number of sellers available willing to take the other side of the trade.

Just observing this price action tells you that at the present moment, the momentum is in favor of the buyers. Prices would not be bid up unless there were fewer sellers in relation to the buyers. If traders continue to pay more and more, the price gets further away from old sellers. Eventually their belief in future value will erode, and one by one the sellers will join the existing pool of buyers competing against one another for the fewer and fewer traders willing to sell. As long as the ratio between buyers and sellers remains as I have just described, there is very little potential for downward price momentum to be established.

Now what will start to tip the balance to cause the market to fall back? For one thing, old buyers will eventually take profits. When they do, they will be joining the existing pool of sellers, thereby increasing the number of traders available to sell. If a move gathers enough steam, it can become similar to a frenzied shark feeding. Eventually, prices will be driven way out of line with some economic factors other traders perceive as relevant compelling them to enter the market in the opposite direction. If these new traders enter with enough force, it will likely cause old buyers to panic adding to the downward momentum.

Maybe you can visualize this back and forth action. When there are more sellers than there are buyers to take the other side of the trade, the balance will be tipped. Sellers will then aggressively offer to sell lower than the last price, responding to what they perceive as a limited number of buyers to take the other side of the trade.

All price movement is a function of group behavior. The market prices flow back and forth like a tug of war between those who believe and expect the market to go up—and consequently buy—and those that believe the market will go lower—and consequently sell.

If there is no balance between the two forces, one side will gain dominance over the other. As prices move farther and farther away from the weak group, the emotional pain of admitting they are wrong will be in direct conflict with their need to avoid losses. Eventually, one by one they will lose faith in their position and liquidate their trade, adding to the momentum of the dominant force.

The prevailing force will continue to dominate until there is a general perception that prices have gone too far and are out of line with other related factors. The members of the dominant force will have to switch sides to liquidate their positions, creating momentum in the opposite direction.

As individuals, if we do not have the strength actually to move prices in the direction we would most benefit from, then the next best thing is to learn to identify and align ourselves with the side that has established dominance until the balance shifts and again align ourselves with the side establishing the strength.

As prices move back and forth in this tug of war, it creates an ebb and flow that is easily identifiable in price charts or point and figure charts. These charts will show us in graphic terms how the forces interact and counteract. They are a visual representation of traders' beliefs in the future and the intensity in which they have been willing to act on those beliefs.

If, for example, a market has been making consistently higher highs and higher lows, to determine what is likely to happen next, ask yourself the following questions:

1. What kind of price action will sustain the buyers' beliefs that they can make more money?

2. When are sellers likely to come into the market in force?

3. Where are old buyers likely to take profits? Where are old sellers likely to lose faith in their positions and bail out?

4. What would have to happen for buyers to lose faith? What would have to happen to draw new buyers into the market?

You can answer all these questions by identifying certain significant reference points where buyers' and or sellers' expectations are likely to be raised and where they are likely to be disappointed if they don't get their way.

Actually, all this works quite nicely in the typical market behavior patterns and price formations with which we are all familiar. So, we are going to look at the psychological makeup of some of these typical patterns. However, before we do, I want to cover a few more definitions.

MARKET BEHAVIOR

The market's behavior can be defined as the collective action of individuals acting in their own self-interest to profit from future price movement while simultaneously creating that movement as an expression of their beliefs about the future.

Behavior patterns result from the collective actions of individual traders doing one of three things: initiating positions, holding positions, and liquidating positions.

What will cause a trader to enter the market? A belief that he can make money and that the current state of the market offers an opportunity to enter into a trade at a price level that is higher or lower than the price at which it can be liquidated.

What will cause a trader to hold a position? A sustained belief that there is still potential for profit in the trade.

What will cause a trader to liquidate a trade? A belief that the market no longer provides an opportunity to make money. This would mean in a winning trade that the market no longer has the potential to move in a direction that will allow the trader to accumulate additional profits or that the risk of staying in the trade is too great in relation to the potential for additional profit. In a losing trade, the trader believes that the market no longer has the potential to move in a direction that will allow him to recover his losses or the trade was a calculated risk in which a predetermined loss level was set in advance.

If you look at any price chart, you notice that over a period of time, prices will form patterns in a very symmetrical fashion. These kinds of symmetrical-looking price patterns are not an accident. They are a visual representation of the struggle between two opposing forces—traders squaring off, so to speak, taking sides and then having to switch sides to liquidate their trades.

Significant Reference Points

Now, what you would be looking for in these charts are significant market reference points. These are defined as anything that causes traders' expectations to be raised about the possibility of something happening. They are points where a large numbers of traders have taken opposing positions. Based on those expectations, they will continue to hold a position in the belief that the expectation will be fulfilled, and most important, they will likely liquidate a position as a result of the expectation being unfulfilled.

Significant reference points are places where the opposing forces (traders with opposite beliefs about the future) have taken a stand, where they have, in their minds, prescribed for the market very limited ways for it to behave, an either/or situation.

The more significant the reference point, the greater the effect traders will have on prices, as the balance of power will shift dramatically between the two opposing forces at these points.

These expectations about what the market will do, projected into price levels, are especially significant because both sides, buyers and sellers, have decided in advance their degree of importance, where one trader is taking one position, betting the market can't or won't do something, and the trader taking the opposite side of the trade is betting that it will.

So, reference points are price levels where many traders on one side of the market are very likely to give up their beliefs about the future, whereas the other side will have their beliefs about the future reinforced. It is where each side expects the market to confirm what they believe to be true. You could say it is a place where the traders' expectations about the future and the future actually meet.

This means for one side, in their minds, that "the market" will make them winners; their beliefs will be validated. All the traders on the other side, however, will be made losers; they will feel the market took something away from them and will naturally be disappointed. I want to point out here that the "objective observer" doesn't care one way or the other; she would just be looking for signs and opportunities.

The greater the expectation traders have about something happening, the less tolerance they have for disappointment. On a collective basis, if you have a whole group of traders who expect something to happen and it doesn't, they will have to trade from the opposite direction of their original trade to get out of their position.

On the other hand, the winners had their beliefs validated, consequently leaving fewer and fewer traders available to let the losers out of their trades. The losers will have to compete among one another for the limited supply of traders willing to take the other side of the trade, the side they originally believed would be successful. For example, if buyers are the losers, they will need other traders to buy from them to get out of their positions. All this activity will result in a great deal of movement in one direction.

Balance Areas

J. Peter Steidlmayer and Kevin Koy in their book *Markets and Market Logic* (Chicago: Porcupine Press, 1987) refer to a "value area," where they discovered that the majority of trading activity on any given day takes place in a normal bell curve distribution pattern. This is very easy to see day after day when you organize trading activity so that you can see how price corresponds with time.

I don't want to get into a lengthy discussion of their methods of organizing market data, which I recommend you learn, other than to distinguish between what they call a "value area" and what I call a "balance area." Steidlmayer and Koy say that most of the trading volume takes place within a specific price range because that range is what the market has established as a fair price representing the value of whatever is being traded.

The distinction I want to make is that the majority of traders don't specifically relate to a fair price or value; they relate to comfort. What gives them comfort is doing what everyone else is doing. In a balance area, traders are basically absorbing each other's orders or energy (their beliefs about the future expressed in the form of energy). When I say that traders relate to comfort, I mean some degree less of the fear they normally feel. Most of the trades take place in a value or balance area because it is where most of the traders feel the least fear, somewhere in the middle of the trading range between an established high or low. This is precisely why there are fewer trades outside the value or balance area and why, as Steidlmayer and Koy say, these trades represent the best opportunities to make money, "to buy or sell away from value." And that is why these are the scariest trades to make because the trader who can make them is all alone; there is no safety in numbers.

There are traders who relate to value by making comparisons between various interrelated contracts and the cash markets. There are the professional commercial or institutional arbitrage traders who will put on or take off positions based on sophisticated mathematical formulas that determine the present value of something as it relates to something else. Otherwise, the majority of traders don't have the slightest concept of value. The more time the market spends at a certain price or in a price range, the more balance, agreement, or comfort there is in the market. Traders are absorbing each other's orders, and nobody is willing to bid the price higher or offer the price lower.

Eventually someone will enter the market who doesn't agree with everyone else and believes there is a possibility for the prices to move much higher or lower. This person or group of traders will basically upset the balance with their buying or selling activity. If their activity is forceful enough, it will set off a series of chain reactions as it causes other traders, who are either holding positions or watching the market for opportunities, to confront these new conditions.

If the balance is tipped in favor of the buyers, for example, it may attract new buyers into the market, creating more buying force and, hence, more disequilibrium. This may cause the traders who are holding short positions to liquidate. To do that they will need to be buyers, leaving fewer and fewer sellers willing to take the other side of the trades the buyers want to get into and the old sellers want to get out of. These traders will compete among one another for the dwindling supply of sellers, bidding the price higher and higher to make it more attractive for someone to sell.

While these traders are in their own little bidding war, they usually lose sight of the fact that the rest of the world is watching what is going on. There could be a trader who is looking to put on a massive hedge to protect the value of an investment portfolio or crop. He is observing this price action from a completely different perspective than the traders on the floor. The floor traders are just concerned with getting their share and not missing out on the opportunity these rapidly rising or falling prices represent. The hedger, on the other hand, is looking at the price rise as an unexpected gift. The rally could have provided much higher prices than he anticipated for locking in the value of something he already owns.

So the commercial trader decides to put on a hedge. And you can assume if one commercial thinks the price is good, others will too. Anyway, if the hedger has an order he perceives to be big enough to stop the rally, he will give instructions to the floor brokers handling his order to do scale in selling, the purpose being to get as much of the order sold as possible without ruining the rally.

However, it won't take long for the other floor traders to figure out what is going on. They are very aware of which floor brokers fill orders for big commercial and institutional customers. Once they find out someone "big" is in the market selling into the rally, few if any of the floor traders will go against them by continuing to buy. No one wants to get caught at the top. So as each group of traders finds out who is selling, they will all try to reverse their positions by selling, and the cycle starts all over again.

Watching this happen from the outside of the pit, it would seem that the reversal is instantaneous, but it isn't. It occurs in waves, as the information about who is selling spreads from the source outward, very much like the waves that result from throwing a stone in a pond.

This leads me to the observation that few traders have any concept of value. They know that price movement creates an opportunity to make money, and it can just as easily take the money away if they don't know what they are doing. If the price trades within a certain range for a period of time, traders will become comfortable with that balance area, making it easier for the trader to trade. As prices move out of the balance area, fewer traders will participate because of what they perceive as more risk than they are comfortable with.

Highs and Lows

Probably the most prominent of these significant reference points are previous highs and lows. If prices are moving steadily higher, buyers will begin to anticipate whether or not prices can penetrate the last high, and sellers will be looking for another top.

In the mind of the seller, that last top, or other tops in the distant past, was a place where the market met enough resistance to stop the rally. In other words, enough traders thought the price was expensive the last time it was there, and they will begin to anticipate whether the same will happen again.

Both buyers and sellers will have raised expectations about the likelihood of the market doing one of two possible things—making new highs or failing to make new highs. As the market approaches this high, if some of them are willing to bid the price past it to some significant level, it could make believers out of other traders who were on the sidelines. If these new traders come into the market as buyers, it will add to the upward momentum, possibly causing old sellers to bail out of their positions. This will also add to the upward momentum of price movement.

Support and Resistance

In a falling market, support is a price level where buyers entered the market or old sellers liquidated their shorts with enough force to keep prices from going any lower. In a rising market, resistance is a price level where sellers entered the market or old buyers liquidated their longs with enough force to keep prices from going any higher.

Support and resistance levels are significant reference points because many traders recognize support and resistance on charts and believe in their significance.

That statement may seem redundant to some people, but it really illustrates a very important point about the nature of the markets (traders acting on their belief in future value). All beliefs eventually become self-fulfilling prophecies. If enough traders believe in the significance of support and resistance, and demonstrate their belief by making trades at those levels, they are in effect fulfilling their own beliefs about the future.

As observers, if we know that each side (in the perpetual tug of war between buyers and sellers) expects one thing to happen, then we will know who will be the winner, who will be the loser, what they will likely do in each case, and how it will affect the balance between the two forces.

For example, if buyers are bidding up a market, causing prices to rise, and all of a sudden many traders are willing to sell for less than the last price (or one trader comes into the market with a big order to sell), causing an immediate price reversal, the price level at which the market stopped is resistance.

Now, it really doesn't matter why the balance of forces shifted from buyers to sellers. Everybody will have his own reasons for what caused prices to reverse. All of them will usually be way beyond the simplest and most obvious reason—that enough traders were displaying a strong enough conviction in their belief in future value to stop the upward price momentum and create downward price momentum.

What is really important about this, however, is that many traders will remember the market reversed at that price level. As a result, that price will then have a degree of significance in the minds of those traders who experienced the reversal.

This first reversal is a top. What we don't know is whether it will remain a top, how long it will take before it is challenged again, or whether it will ever be challenged again.

If the buyers are dominant enough to bid the market back up to the previous high, they will consider this second attempt a test and begin to anticipate whether or not prices can exceed the previous high. The only way that can happen is if these higher prices actually attract additional traders into the market on the buy side because they believe it is an opportunity to buy low relative to the future. Floor traders are especially aware of whether or not new traders are being attracted into the market from off the floor and act on this information.

For the sake of this example, if the market reversed very strongly the last time prices approached this level, there will be many traders who will think it will probably reverse again. As a result, they may act on their belief about the low probability of prices trading beyond the last high and thereby prevent it from happening. If more traders are willing to act on the belief that it won't in relation to those who act on the belief that it will, then prices will stop again.

Technically, once the market tests a previous high or low and fails to penetrate, you then have a defined support and resistance area. Support and resistance are most easily identified in point-and-figure charts because they graphically represent price movement in reversals. Once support and resistance are established and identified, it can be very easy to trade by putting your orders on either side of the support or resistance line.

For example, if over the last two weeks, every time the bonds rallied to 95-25, then fell back significantly to some support level, like 94-10, what I have just described is a support and resistance zone, commonly referred to as a trading range. The significance of either end of the zone would be determined by how many times prices rallied to 95-25 and failed to penetrate, and how many times prices fell to 94-10 and failed to penetrate. Obviously, the more attempts and failures, the more weight these points will have in the minds of the traders who experience these tests and subsequent failures.

For an objective observer with no bias toward any particular direction, trading ranges can be very easy ways to make money. As the market approaches 95-25, put in an order to sell somewhere around 95-21. Since we know the markets are not precise, you don't want to put your order exactly at the upper end of the range, because each time the market makes an attempt to penetrate there will be many traders who will be anticipating a failure. As a result, they will start selling early and the price may never get to 95-25 for you to get filled, if you had placed your order there.

Also, put an order in the market to stop and reverse (buy two) possibly around 95-31. Each circumstance will be different. In this example, the 6 ticks that I have given the market to define itself may not be enough. The object would be to put your orders in a place where the highest probability is that it will continue in the direction of your trade. If the market trades to 95-31, it still may not be enough for old sellers to become disappointed and bail out of their positions en masse, causing prices to rise even further.

This trade will work if the resistance level has a high degree of significance in the minds of enough traders for them to act and sell against it in relation to those who are willing buy. Each time the market approaches this area, traders will expect either one of two possible things to happen. The market will penetrate, or it will fail again. In any case the price move that results will be significant because one side of the market will be disappointed. And if we know what will validate and disappoint each group, then we can determine how they will likely behave and thereby affect the balance of the market.

Since the market can display billions of combinations of behaviors from one point to the next, significant reference points like support and resistance narrow those behaviors down to two likely possibilities. By putting your order on both sides, you can take advantage of the situation, regardless of what happens.

Support Becomes Resistance and Resistance Becomes Support

Many traders have read or heard that old support becomes resistance and old resistance becomes support. This bit of market insight is valid for some very sound psychological reasons.

If resistance has been established at 95-25, it is because there were enough traders who sold at that price to make it resistance. In fact, it would probably be the same group of traders who sold at 95-25 each time the market approached that price. So, every time the market rallied up to 95-25 and sold off, it made winners out of all those traders who chose to sell at or near that price. As a result, 95-25 will take on a great deal of significance in the minds of the traders who were successful. Each subsequent time they are successful will only strengthen their belief and faith in that price level.

Now, the prices rally up to 95-25 again, maybe for the fourth or fifth time, and like the last time, you will have a group of traders who believe in that resistance level and will sell against it. Only this time the buyers are very strong on the way up and continue to buy right on through the resistance level.

All the traders who choose to sell at 95-25 are now faced with having to deal with a losing trade. Some will get out with a small loss, others will hang on hoping the market will come back. In any case, the market invalidated their beliefs about the future, and they are suffering considerably. They had faith in 95-25, and in their minds the market betrayed them.

If the market happens to come back to 95-25 after rallying for several days, how do you think the group of traders who sold at 95-25 the last time—the ones who believe they were betrayed—are going to behave? First, the traders who were hanging on in hopes of the market coming back will bail out as soon as they are close to being made whole. They are so grateful for getting their money back, there is no way they will stay in that trade regardless of what the possibilities are for additional profits. They will have to be buyers to liquidate their shorts and will be all too happy to end their suffering.

The traders who originally cut their losses when the market blew through 95-25 won't consider selling at that price again because of the emotional pain of being wrong the last time they sold at that price. I am not saying they will in turn be buyers at that level, but they are very likely not to sell. The overall effect this will have on the balance of the market is to take away from the existing pool of available sellers at 95-25 (old resistance), thereby causing the balance to be tipped in favor of the buyers. Hence, old resistance becomes support, and old support becomes resistance for the same reasons.

Trends and Trendlines

Trends, a series of higher highs and higher lows, or lower highs and lower lows over a period of time, work because there aren't enough sellers to absorb the number of buyers competing with each other to get into the market during that period of time. Adding to this buying force will be old sellers at lower levels who finally lose faith and bail out of their positions. They will do this in significant numbers when the prices penetrate what they believe to be significant reference points.

Keep in mind that trends are a function of time. The next tick up could be defined as a one-tick trend. How long will the imbalance between buyers and sellers last?

In an upward-trending market, prices will retrace because buyers are taking profits. This will create some counteracting pressure, but if the trend continues after a normal retracement, it just tells you there still aren't enough sellers around to absorb all the buyers, with enough left over to create downward momentum. You will know when that has happened when the trending market breaks its normal ebb and flow pattern. That is why markets that break trendlines have a tendency to keep on going in the direction of the break, because it signals a significant shift in the balance of forces.

After a certain period of time, you can notice how trending markets will develop a certain rhythm and flow, making the price movement look very symmetrical on a bar chart. You really don't have to know why this is so, you just have to notice that it exists. When this flow is broken (the market trading above or below a significant trend line), it is a good indication the balance of the market forces has shifted. Then ask yourself, what is the likelihood the shift will gain hold and continue trending in the direction of the break?

You don't even have to know the answer to that question. Put in an order at a spot that would confirm the highest probability of a change in the balance. Then wait for the market to define itself. If your order is filled, put a stop where the market shouldn't be to confirm that your trade is still valid. "What is a valid trade?" you ask. One where the highest probabilities for price movement are in the direction of the prevailing force.

High $\longrightarrow$ Retrace $\longrightarrow$ Rally to a Lower High

I will give you an example. No matter how simple a trade this is, it has very sound psychological reasons for working. In this example, the market made new highs and sold off. The sell-off could be the result of new sellers coming into the market in force, or old buyers selling to take their profits, or a combination of both. Prices will continue to drop until enough traders believe the price is cheap and are willing to take the initiative and bid the price back up. As the price approaches the last previous high, buyers will begin to anticipate whether or not prices can penetrate, and sellers will be looking for another top.

In either case expectations by both will be raised. If some buyers are willing to bid the price past the previous highs to some significant level, it will make believers out of others who were on the sidelines. If they do come in, it will add to the momentum.

Some old sellers will admit to being wrong and will have to buy to get out of their trades, thus adding to the upward momentum.

However, what if the market approaches the highs the second time, and sellers come back into the market again with enough force to keep the price from exceeding or equaling the previous high? Buyers will start to become disappointed. Where will they really be disappointed?—if enough buyers don't come into the market to support the price at the previous low. If prices penetrate that low, watch for buyers to bail out en masse. For them to get out of their position, who is going to buy it from them? If everybody is trying to sell and no one is available to buy, what are prices going to do? Fall like a rock.

The reason why a bull market is ready to turn into a bear market when the general public gets involved is because the general public has the least tolerance for risk and consequently needs the most reassurance and confirmation that what they are doing is a sure thing. As a result, they will be the last to be convinced that the rising market represents an opportunity. If a bull market has lasted for any length of time, the general public will feel compelled to jump on the bandwagon so to speak, because of their perception that everyone else is doing it and making money. They will pick up on any reason that sounds the most rational to justify their participation, when in reality, they will know very little about what they are doing, but since everyone else is doing it, how can they go wrong.

A continuing bull market requires the continual infusion of new traders who are willing to pay higher and higher prices. The longer a bull market lasts, the greater the number of people who are already participating as buyers, leaving fewer and fewer traders who haven't already bought and fewer and fewer traders who are willing to bid the price up. These older buyers obviously want to see the market keep on going up, but they also don't want to get caught holding the bag, if the market stops going up. As their profits accumulate from the higher prices, they start to get nervous about taking their profits.

By the time the general public starts buying en masse, the professional traders knows the end is near. How does the professional know this? Because the professional knows that there is a practical limit to the number of people who will participate to bid the price up. There will come a point where everyone who is likely to be a buyer will have already bought, quite literally leaving no one else to buy. The professional trader would like the market to continue to go up indefinitely just like all the other buyers. However, he also understands the impracticality of that happening, so he starts taking his profits while there are still some buyers available to sell to. When the last buyer has bought, the market has no place to go but down.

The public gets stuck because they weren't willing to take the risk when there was still potential for the market to move. For the market to sustain itself, it needs to attract more and more people. As big as this country is or the world for that matter, there are only so many people who will buy. Eventually the supply of buyers runs out, and when it does the market falls like a rock.

The professionals have been selling out their positions before this happens, but once the supply of buyers runs out, the professionals start to compete among one another for the available supply of buyers which is dwindling fast, so they offer lower and lower prices to attract someone into the market so they can get out. At some point, instead of the lower prices being attractive to people, it panics them. The public didn't anticipate losing. Their expectations are very high with very little toleration for disappointment. The only reason they got in was because it was a sure thing. When the public starts to sell, it starts a stampede.

Again, people will ascribe their actions to some rational reason because nobody wants to be thought of as irrational and panic-stricken. The real reason why people panicked and the prices fell is simply because prices didn't keep on going up.

CHAPTER 16

The Steps to Success

Self-discipline is simply a mental technique to stay focused on what you need to learn, or do, to accomplish your goals. There will be times when you won't have the resources to function effectively relative to the external conditions. Other times the resources you do have will be in conflict with both the conditions and your goals. So to accomplish your goals, you will need to adapt. In other words, you will need to change the way you interact with the environment. To change your behavior and how you experience the environment (feelings and emotions), you will have to change your perspective. To change your perspective, you will have to change the mental components that effect your perception of environmental information. Keep in mind that you can't physically control what the markets do; you can only learn to control your perception of the markets to share the highest degree of reality (the least amount of distortion) with everyone else who is participating or has the potential to participate.

The more sophisticated you become as a trader, the more you will realize that trading is completely mental. It isn't you against the markets, it's just you. All the other traders participating to make the market provide you with an opportunity to make money from their divergent beliefs about the future. If people didn't disagree about the future value of any particular commodity or stock, then there would be nothing to compel them to either bid a price higher or offer it lower, and the opportunity to profit from these changes would cease to exist. So the markets just offer the individual trader opportunity. They don't choose the data on which you focus your attention, and they certainly don't interpret the data you perceive. Nor are the markets responsible for what you can't perceive because of the distinctions you haven't learned to make yet. They also don't choose when you put on a trade, how long you stay in, when you get out, or how many contracts you buy or sell.

Each individual trader creates his own experience of the markets based on this picking and choosing process and the decisions that result. If you accept this concept as valid, then the implications are that you will never have a valid reason to blame the markets for your unsatisfying results. The markets don't owe you anything (regardless of how hard you work to be successful) because every other trader participating is doing so to take your money away. You and you alone are completely responsible for whatever you end up with. The sooner you accept that responsibility (if you haven't already), the easier it will be to identify what skills you need to learn to interact with the markets more successfully. Even if you can't identify the mental components responsible for what you ended up with, at least by assuming that you are responsible, you will be opening yourself up to find out.

To be a successful trader you need to trade without fear. As you have already learned when you use fear as a resource to limit yourself, you will create the very conditions you are trying to avoid. Or to say this another way, you will experience your fears. You also can't learn anything new because fear will force you to perceive the environmental "now" from your individual past. You will experience that past regardless of the opportunities the environment may have to offer in that same moment. Your individual history will repeat itself until you change your history, which will then allow you to learn and experience something new. Evolving beyond your fears is also the best way to learn how to predict market behavior. The more fearful traders are, the fewer the choices they perceive as available to themselves and the easier it is to predict their behavior. You will be able to recognize this clearly in others when you recognize it yourself and work your way out of the condition where you trade with fear.

However, you will need some resource to limit yourself so that you don't get reckless. Getting reckless is exactly what people have a tendency to do if they don't feel any fear, especially if there is a potential for thrilling results, as there is in trading. The resource you need to limit yourself is self-trust. You will gain that self-trust when you establish a set of rules and guidelines to trade by and know that you will always follow those rules without hesitation, regardless of the temptations to do otherwise.

Once you trust yourself to always do what needs to be done, there will be nothing to fear because the markets won't be able to do anything to you, as a result of your inability to respond appropriately. Consequently, with nothing to fear, you are then free to observe the markets free of distortions. There won't be any need to avoid certain categories of information because of how that information will make you feel. The less reason you have to avoid or distort information, the more you make yourself available to learn about the nature of the markets. The more you learn, the easier it will be to anticipate what the market will do next. If you can accurately anticipate what will happen next, the easier it will be to give yourself more and more money (notwithstanding any mental components that would argue against giving yourself more money).

It is very important for you to understand that these new insights about the market's behavior will come in stages as you learn to trust yourself more and more. There is no "get rich quick" scheme being offered here. There are enough rags to riches to rags stories to attest to the fact that get rich quick doesn't work anyway. Getting rich quick can only lead to a great deal of anxiety and frustration if you don't have the skills to keep it. There isn't much point to making a lot of money if you are a susceptible to making that one trading error that can give it all back plus more. Once you have made a fortune and lost it, the psychological work that you will need to do to get it back is enormous compared to work that is necessary to keep yourself from losing it in the first place. *As a trader it is more important to know that you will always follow your rules than it is to make money, because whatever money you make, you will inevitably lose back to the market if you can't follow your rules.*

You also need to understand that your rules will change as your understanding and insights evolve. Many people don't like to establish trading rules because they believe that once made, they can't be changed. Any exercise that I offer you or rule that you select to guide your trading behavior is only transitory. They are methods and techniques to get you beyond certain fundamental stages of development so that you can recognize for yourself their value and what you need to do next to be more successful. In fact, a good rule of thumb to use to determine your readiness to move beyond a certain rule or exercise and to the next challenge is the recognition that you can do what you set out to learn so well that it becomes second nature. Otherwise, keep working at it until you don't have to think about it any longer.

STEP ONE: STAYING FOCUSED ON WHAT YOU NEED TO LEARN

First and foremost, you may need to change your perspective or the focus of your trading. Until now your focus may have been to make money. If this is so, you will need to change your perspective to "What do I need to learn or how will I have to adapt myself to interact more successfully?" You need to stay focused on mastering the steps to achieving your goal and not the end result, knowing that the end result, money, will be a by-product of what you know and how well you can act on what you know.

There is a tremendous difference between focusing on money and focusing on using your trading as an exercise to identify what you need to learn. The first will cause you to focus on what the markets are giving you or are taking away from you. The second perspective causes you to focus your attention on your ability to to give yourself money. With the first perspective, you are placing some of the responsibility onto the markets to do something for you. With the second perspective, you assume all the responsibility.

Always keep in mind that each moment is a perfect reflection of your level of development. If you look at each moment that things don't turn out as you want or expect as a mistake, then you will usually cut yourself off from the insight about yourself contained within each moment. The reason why we will cut ourselves off from this information is because we typically associate mistakes with pain. We will instinctively avoid pain and in doing so also avoid what we need to know about ourselves to interact more effectively in similar circumstances in the future.

To evolve beyond pain and our fear of mistakes, our mistakes have to be resolved. This could be a big task and you may not want to tackle it at this time. So what you will need to do is build a corollary framework to place all of your trading experiences. This framework needs to be defined in such a way that all experiences are valid and have meaning, and, as such, mistakes don't exist—they just point the way.

As part of this framework you may also need to change your definition of a missed opportunity. Except for the inability to accept a loss, there isn't anything that has the potential to cause more psychological damage than a belief in missed opportunities. Missed opportunities are trades that would have always turned out perfectly because they only occurred in our minds, where we can make anything be as we want it to be. Of course, we would have responded exactly as the conditions warranted without flaw. The problem is we didn't do it, and the resulting sense of loss we feel is difficult to reconcile. Therefore, these missed opportunity trades have the potential to cause more anxiety and stress than the trades we actually do take that turn out to be losers.

Nothing's worse than missing a "perfect" opportunity. However, if you could have, you would have; it's that simple. The sooner you accept this, the sooner you will be able to take advantage of these missed opportunities instead of beating yourself up over them. Besides there really isn't anything to miss because the markets are in perpetual motion and will continue to be until everyone agrees on value. As long as the price keeps changing, there will always be another opportunity.

When you start trading from the perspective that mistakes don't exist, you will be amazed at the sense of freedom you will feel to grow by accepting your results as a reflection of who you are in that moment, which then allows you to determine what you need to learn to do better. When you release the energy out of the belief that it is possible to miss anything, you will no longer feel compelled to do something, like getting into trades too early or too late. In other words, you will be giving yourself additional choices (not doing something is often the most appropriate choice) where only one choice existed.

You need to constantly keep in mind that the professional traders from whom you are trying to extract money already know and are using many of the principles put forth in this book. They understand the concept of objectivity, have learned how to trade without fear, and know how to execute their trades properly. Before you can begin to take money out of the markets consistently instead of the markets taking yours, you will also have to learn these skills.

So, I would suggest that you set aside a certain amount of trading capital as tuition for your education. How much you set aside will be a function of how many skills you need to learn. What is most important is that you make a firm commitment to your education as a trader. Even if you have been trading for years and you are successful, but not as successful as you would like to be, setting aside money that you will trade with as an exercise to learn some needed skill is a very powerful symbol of your commitment to learning that skill. The stronger your commitment, the faster you will learn.

STEP TWO: DEALING WITH LOSSES

Trading Rule 1

Predefine what a loss is in every potential trade. By "predefine," I mean determine what the market has to look like or do, to tell you that the trade no longer represents an opportunity, at least not an opportunity in the time frame in which you trade.

When your beliefs about losses are restructured, the possibility of a losing trade will not create any threat of pain. Most successful traders restructured their beliefs about losses after they lost one or more fortunes. They experienced their worst fears about losing and then came to the realization that they didn't have anything to fear if they just did what needs to be done. What needs to be done? Confront the possibility of being wrong and consequently not avoid the inevitability of taking a loss. So confronting and accepting the inevitability of a loss is a trading skill, certainly a skill learned the hard way for most, but nevertheless an essential component at the foundation of virtually everything you need to learn to become a successful trader.

The relatively few successful traders in the market today did it the hard way. You, on the other hand, have the opportunity to do it much more easily. There will be two mental components at work to help you acquire this skill. First is *your understanding* of why it is so essential to confront the possibility of a loss. If you don't, you will generate fear and end up creating the very experience that you are trying to avoid. When you really understand this concept, it will become unacceptable to you to trade from the old perspective of loss avoidance.

The second is *your willingness* to change your definitions of what it means to lose. By using some of the mental exercises in Chapter 14 you can change these definitions by using your thoughts instead of having to lose everything or practically everything you own to get to the same place. That place is "losses do not diminish me (you) as a person." The sooner you believe it, the easier it will be to identify and execute a losing trade. By making the execution of a losing trade an automatic function of your trading strategy, you make yourself psychologically available to take advantage of the next opportunity, even if that opportunity is in the same direction of the losing trade you just got out of.

Trading Rule 2

Execute your losing trades immediately upon perception that they exist. When losses are predefined and executed without hesitation, there is nothing to consider, weigh, or judge and consequently nothing to tempt yourself with. There will be no threat of allowing yourself the possibility of ultimate disaster. If you find yourself considering, weighing, or judging, then you are either not predefining what a loss is or you are not executing them immediately upon perception, in which case, if you don't and it turns out to be profitable, you are reinforcing an inappropriate behavior that will inevitably lead to disaster. Or if you don't and the loss worsens, you will create a negative cycle of pain, that once started will be difficult to stop. The next error after letting a loss get out of hand is usually not taking the next opportunity, which invariably is always a winning trade. After which, we get so angry at ourselves for passing up that opportunity that we make ourselves susceptible to any number of other trading errors, like taking a trade that was a tip from another trader, which invariably is always a loser.

It is important for you to note that once you completely trust yourself to cut your losses, you will eventually get to the point where you may not have to predefine what a loss is. There are traders who have reached such a high degree of objectivity and trust that they can get into a trade and know when it is a loser without having to predefine it for themselves. They let the market define it for them based on their comprehensive knowledge of the various participants involved and their knowledge of the various relationships between price movement and time. However, the reason why they were able to learn what they know about the nature of the markets is because their focus of attention widened to include more undistorted information leading to greater insights, once they learned, first, however, to trust themselves. Keep in mind, that fear is really the only thing that keeps us from learning anything new. You can't learn anything new about the nature of the market's behavior if you are afraid of what you may do or can't do that is not in your best interests. *By predefining and cutting your losses short, you are making yourself available to learn the best possible way to let your profits grow.*

STEP THREE: BECOMING AN EXPERT AT JUST ONE MARKET BEHAVIOR

Generally, most of us grow up believing that when we have to make a decision, the more relevant information we can gather, the better our decisions will be. This isn't necessarily true with trading, especially in the beginning stages of one's career. In most market situations, there is an even number of traders who have a propensity to buy and those who have a propensity to sell or those who need to buy and want someone to take the other side of the transaction and vice versa. Everyone will have his reasons and rationalizations for all this trading activity, creating about as much conflicting information as there are participants. Because there is so much information and because so much of that information is conflicting, the beginning trader will need specifically to limit his awareness of the market information to which he allows himself to be exposed. More is not better; it just creates confusion and overload that will ultimately lead to losses.

You need to start as small as possible and then gradually allow yourself to grow into greater and greater amounts of market information. What you want to do is become an expert at just one particular type of behavior pattern that repeats itself with some degree of frequency. To become an expert, choose one simple trading system that identifies a pattern, preferably one that is mechanical, instead of mathematical, so that you will be working with a visual representation of market behavior. Your objective is to understand completely every aspect of the system—all the relationships between the components—and its potential to produce profitable trades. In the meantime, it is important to avoid all other possibilities and information.

Out of all the combinations of behavior possible, you are going to limit your focus of attention to just one combination. Consequently, you will be letting all the other opportunities go by. Starting small and gradually working into other combinations is a real exercise in discipline that has a couple of important psychological benefits. First, you will be building a base of confidence as you learn that you can, in fact, accurately assess what will most likely happen next. It is much easier to gain this confidence if you don't overwhelm yourself with the market's seemingly infinite possibilities. Second, by passing up other opportunities that you are not an expert at yet, you will be releasing yourself from any compelling desire to trade. Any compelling behavior is usually the result of some fear. That fear, in turn, will cause you to behave in many inappropriate ways.

If the idea of letting go of opportunities that don't fit into your framework is troubling to you, then ask yourself, what is the rush? If you are confident in your ability to transform yourself into a successful trader, what difference could it make that you let go of some opportunities now for educational purposes? Once you learn to become the trader you want to be, you can then give yourself as much money as you desire. However, to get to that point, your objective should be to plan your development in such a way that you do the least amount of damage to yourself, both financially and psychologically. Then after you have developed the appropriate skills, taking money out of the markets can be as easy as almost everyone believes it is before he started trading.

If, on the other hand, you end up doing a lot of damage to yourself, you will have to undo that damage before you can accumulate wealth as a trader. After the damage is done, it won't make any difference how much you learn about the nature of the markets or how well you learn to perceive an opportunity. There are many traders who end up becoming expert market analysts but can't make a dime as traders because of all the damage they did to themselves in the early part of their trading careers. What happens in these situations is a trader's "past" will generate so much fear that he won't be able execute his trades properly or not at all, regardless of how well he learned to predict what the market will do next. Nothing is more frustrating than to know what is going to happen next and not be able to do anything about it.

You need to understand that the ability to perceive an opportunity, based on the quality of distinctions that you can make and your ability to execute a trade, are not automatic functions of one another. Perception and execution are separate skills. They can and do work in tandem, if there are no mental components blocking execution. Otherwise, the "intent" to take advantage of what you perceive as an opportunity may not have any inner support or the kind of inner support that is necessary to execute your intent properly. If there are mental obstacles preventing the proper execution of a trade, then learning how to perceive better opportunities is not going to solve the problem.

So the object of this exercise is to help you learn how become an expert and stay healthy while you are doing it. And when you do become one, there will be much less standing in the way of your taking maximum advantage of your perceptive skills. If you are already looking at or trading several markets and you are not successful or not as successful as you desire, then I would suggest that you scale back to just one market or two at the most. Don't expand until you thoroughly understand the markets' characteristics.

STEP FOUR: LEARNING HOW TO EXECUTE A TRADING SYSTEM FLAWLESSLY

The proper execution of your trades is one of the most fundamental components of becoming a successful trader and probably the most difficult to learn. It is certainly much easier to identify something in the market that represents an opportunity than it is to act upon it. However, there are some good reasons why it is so difficult to act on a trading signal other than what has already been identified as mental obstacles. To understand these reasons, you need to understand the nature of trading systems (defined as any methodology that consistently identifies an opportunity to buy or sell with a potential profit in some future moment), and how they interact with the markets and ourselves.

Most good trading systems, technical or otherwise, will take consistent money out of the markets over the long run. Many of these good systems have been available to the public for years, and yet, there is still a huge gap between what is possible and what almost everyone ends up with. The problem with trading systems is they define market behavior in limited ways when the market can behave in an infinite combination of ways. Systems mathematically or mechanically reduce relationships in human behavior characteristics to percentage odds of what could happen next. They can only capture a very limited number of these behavior characteristics compared to the billions that are possible. Any identified pattern may or may not be repeating itself with respect to the way the pattern or relationship progressed when it was observed in the past. Therefore, we never really know if it is valid or not until it has actually completed itself. The big psychological problem here is that people have difficulty acting on opportunities with probable outcomes.

Most people like to think of themselves as risk takers, but what they really want is a guaranteed outcome with some momentary suspense to make them feel as if the outcome had been in doubt. The momentary suspense adds the thrill factor necessary to keep our lives from getting too boring. When it comes right down to it, no one trades to lose, no one puts on a trade believing it is going to be a loser, and all systems will definitely have some percentage of losing trades. So it's difficult not to be tempted into trying to guess which ones are going to be the losers and not participate.

As most of you reading this book already know, trying to outguess your trading system is an exercise in extreme frustration. Sometimes the system will give you signals to trade in ways that are completely contrary to your logic and reasoning. Sometimes the system will defy your reasoning and be right, and sometimes you will agree with the system and it will be wrong. You need to understand that technical trading systems are not designed to be outguessed. What I mean is, they aren't designed to give you isolated signals of an opportunity to be taken when it seems right. What they do is mathematically define, quantify, and categorize past relationships in collective human behavior to give you a statistically probable outcome of the future.

As a comparison to trading, it is much easier to take risks and participate in a gambling event with a purely random outcome based on statistical probabilities, simply because it is random. What I mean is, if you risk your money on a gambling event that you know has a random outcome, then there's no rational way you could have predicted what that outcome would be. Therefore, you don't have to take responsibility for the outcome if it isn't positive.

Whereas, with trading, the future is not random, price movement, opportunity, and outcomes are created by traders acting on their beliefs and expectations of the future. Every trader contributes to the outcome of the future by putting on and taking off trades in accordance with their beliefs. Because traders actually create the future by collectively acting on their beliefs about the future, the outcome of their actions is not exactly random. Why else would traders try to outguess their systems, unless they had some concept of the future and how that future will affect the markets?

This adds an element of responsibility to trading that doesn't exist with a purely random event and that is difficult to avoid. This higher degree of responsibility means that more of your self-esteem is at stake, making it much more difficult to participate. Trading gives you all kinds of ways to beat yourself up for all of the things you should have or could have considered that would have resulted in a more satisfying outcome.

Furthermore, you don't trade in an information vacuum. You form your expectations about the future with information technical systems don't take into consideration. Consequently, this sets up a conflict between what your intellect says should be happening and the purely mathematical means of predicting human behavior afforded by your technical system. This is precisely why technical systems are so difficult to relate to and execute. People aren't taught to think in terms of probabilities—and we certainly don't grow up constructing a conceptual framework that correlates a prediction of mass human behavior in statistical odds by means of a mathematical formula.

To be able to execute your trading systems properly, you will need to incorporate two concepts into your mental framework—thinking in terms of probabilities and correlating the numbers or the mechanics of your system to the behavior. Unfortunately, the only way you can really learn these things is actually to experience them by executing your system. The problem is that rarely will the typical trader stay with his system beyond two or three losses in a row, and taking two or three losses in a row is a very common occurrence for most trading systems. This creates something of a paradox or Catch 22. How do you do it if you don't believe it, and you won't learn to believe it unless you do it long enough for it to become a part of your mental framework? This is where you employ mental discipline to make flawless execution a habit.

Exercise

Take some of the trading capital that you set aside for your education to buy and trade a simple trading system with well-defined entry and exit points. Make a commitment to trade this system exactly according to the rules. You need to make a very strong commitment here and not play any games with yourself. The object of this exercise is to work through any resistance you may have to following your rules.

This system does not have to be expensive. You can get one out of many of the books on technical analysis available today. I think it is important to buy one instead of devising one of your own because it might be a little easier to stay focused on the objectives of this exercise. With any system you devise, you are naturally going to want to make money. Save it for later, after you have learned how to execute properly.

You also need to find a system that suits your unique tolerance for taking a loss. The amount of money you risk per trade should be an amount that you are completely comfortable with, at least at first. If you don't stay within this tolerance level, you will be, at the very least, uncomfortable, in which case to whatever degree you are uncomfortable, you shut down the learning process. When you are feeling pain, instead of being focused on what the market is teaching you about itself and yourself, you will be focused on information that will ease your pain. Which usually results in a painful lesson.

Your objectives are to (1) learn the skill of flawless execution by learning that you can follow the rules you set forth for yourself (I am defining "flawless execution" as executing a trade immediately upon perception of an opportunity; inclusive within opportunity is the opportunity to exit a losing trade.) and (2) to incorporate a belief into your mental system about the nature of probable outcomes so that you believe that you can make money in the long run with your trading system, if, of course, you can execute it properly.

You will likely encounter many beliefs arguing against flawless execution. Here are few suggestions to help you work through this resistance:

First, understand that this exercise (at least for most people) is not going to be easy, so be easy on yourself. The more accepting you are of your mistakes, the easier it will be to make the next attempt. If your child were learning how to ride a bike, I'm sure you wouldn't scold him for falling off and tell him not to try again. You would encourage him and eventually he'd learn. Give yourself the same kind of understanding and consideration.

Second, taking *all* the signals generated by your system is the only way you can get the firsthand experience you need to establish a belief in probable outcomes, and relating the mathematics or the mechanics to the behavior. You have to do it in spite of your resistance, and you have to do it long enough for the system to become a part of your mental framework. When that happens, you will have the force of habit working for you, and the struggle will cease. Just do the best you can and look for ways to improve your performance. Constantly keep in mind that what you are doing is more of an exercise in learning trading discipline and the skill of flawless execution, which in the long run is far more important than your immediate desire to make money. So keep your contract size light. You can always increase it later, when you have learned to trust yourself completely to always do what needs to be done without hesitation.

Stay with the exercise until it becomes second nature or a part of who you are. As you gain in your confidence, you will learn more and consequently learn how to make money as a trader. As you make money you will gain in your confidence. This positive cycle will expand your ability to be successful just as easily as a negative cycle will feed on itself to end in despair.

STEP FIVE: LEARNING TO THINK
IN PROBABILITIES

After you have mastered the more fundamental skills, in other words, once you have acquired the discipline necessary to interact with the trading environment effectively, you can start to use your reasoning skills and intuitive powers to determine what the market is likely to do next. This will entail learning to think in probabilities. What I mean by this is, if you can't personally move the market, then you will want to be able to identify the group that is demonstrating the greatest possibility of moving the market and you will want to trade with that group. Or you will want to determine the prevalent beliefs being expressed in the market and how those beliefs will affect price movement. That identification process requires a detached objective perspective, where you are watching and listening to what the market is telling you, instead of being focused on what the market is doing to you personally.

Remember, two traders willing to trade at a price make a market. Whatever the extreme ends of human expression are is what the market is capable of doing. For example, have you ever said, "The market can't break contract lows, it's never been there before"? If you bought those lows based on your belief of its impossibility, then consider that all it takes is one trader who is willing to sell lower to make you wrong. The fact that the market did it makes it right. You could have been a seller at the all-time lows and been a one-tick winner when the next trader broke those lows, if you could have perceived selling as an opportunity.

If prices were to penetrate those lows with any kind of followthrough, it would indicate that there are plenty of traders who believe it wasn't going higher. These sellers obviously acted on their beliefs with enough force to outnumber the buyers available to take the other side of the trade. Regardless of the criteria the sellers used to justify their actions, how rational or irrational by anyone else's standards, nothing will alter the fact the market traded lower. The fact that you believed it couldn't do it is of no consequence, unless you can trade big enough numbers to reverse it. Otherwise, you can either be with it or against it.

To help you learn how to be with the flow of the market, I pose a series of questions that are designed to keep you focused in the "now moment" to determine what is true about the market.

1. What is the market telling me at this moment?
2. Who is paying up to get in or get out?
3. How much strength is there?
4. Is momentum building?
5. Can it be measured relative to something?
6. What would have to happen to indicate the momentum is changing?
7. Is the trend weakening or is this a normal retracement?
8. What would show that? If the market has displayed a fairly symmetrical type of pattern and that pattern has been disturbed, then it is a good indication the balance of forces has shifted.
9. Are there any places where one side will definitely gain dominance over the other? If that point is reached, it still may take sometime for the other side to be convinced they are losers. How long are you willing to give them to stampede out of their positions?
10. If they don't stampede out of their positions, what will that tell you?
11. What did traders have to believe to form the current pattern relative to the past? Remember that people's beliefs don't change easily unless they are extremely disappointed. People are disappointed when their expectations aren't fulfilled.
12. What will disappoint the predominate force?
13. What is the likelihood of that happening?
14. What is the risk of finding out in a trade?
15. Is there enough potential for movement to make the trade worth the risk?

We may never know what traders will in fact do. But we can determine what they will likely do if certain things happen first. For example, if traders push the price lower than the previous low, what will likely occur? Is this new low significant enough to cause traders holding long positions to bail out? Will it cause new shorts to enter the market or attract existing shorts to add to their positions? New shorts may be attracted to the market, and old shorts will add to their position. This price slide will stop when enough traders believe the price is cheap relative to something. That reference point will likely be some other previous old high or low.

If you can't determine the significance of any particular high or low or any other significant reference point for that matter, then you have to ask yourself if it is worth the risk of finding out. How much room will you have to give the market to define itself before it is evident that the flow of the market is not in the direction of that trade?

Ask yourself this question: For this trade to be valid or continue to be valid, the market shouldn't trade to what point? If it trades within that point, then the trade still has potential for working. Beyond that point, it is no longer valid in the direction that I started.

Keep in mind that the amount of price movement that you determine is necessary for the market to define itself has to correspond with your emotional tolerance to accept the dollar value of a loss that size. Otherwise, don't take the trade regardless of how much potential you think it might have, unless you can realistically change the foregoing parameters to fit your capacity for a potential loss.

Let the market define itself and then apply whatever criteria you use to define an opportunity. Identify your significant reference points and place your orders on either side of the point; then wait for the market to do whatever it is going to do. Try putting your orders in the market in advance of whatever you perceive as having a high probability of occurring based on the existing market conditions. By putting your orders in advance of some anticipated move, you will be learning how to let the market work for you. Placing your orders in advance will also help to keep you from having an opinion, and you won't be subjecting yourself to the moment-to-moment conflict inherent within all price movement.

Keep in mind that since the market is in perpetual motion, it puts you in a position of having to make never-ending assessments of the current risk in relationship to the current possibilities for reward. To do this effectively, you will have to learn to observe the market as if you were not in a position. This perspective will free you to take whatever action is appropriate for the situation instead of hesitating, hoping, and wishing that the market will make you right.

The market doesn't make you right, you make yourself right. Your inability to execute or the degree to which you hesitate after you perceive an opportunity to get in or out of a trade or reverse your position will be an excellent gauge as to how locked in you are mentally. Making note of these occurrences of hesitation or immobility will give you an indication of the exact state of your mental resources to execute. You need this information to use as a reference point to build from.

When you are about to enter into a position, ask yourself, by imagining, what the next five minutes or tomorrow (depending on your time frame) would have to look like to validate your trade, to confirm that the trend is still intact. What would the next five minutes or tomorrow have to look like to indicate the opposite. Then, again, place your orders at the appropriate price in advance of the market's getting there.

All these questions will keep reminding you that anything can happen, and you will be preparing yourself in advance for those possibilities. Also, if anything can happen, then of course, you will have to consider that there will always be something you haven't taken into consideration, had absolutely no awareness of or could have no prior knowledge of, for example, such as how many traders may enter the market for the first time with enough force to reverse its direction.

Keep in mind that prices move in the direction of the greatest force (traders fulfilling their beliefs about the future). Or said in its converse form, prices will move in the direction of the least resistance to the prevailing force. Significant reference points give you the opportunity to make high probability assessments of the degree of balance or imbalance between the two forces, the point at which it is likely to shift, and in whose favor.

By learning to identify significant reference points, you can determine what each group will do based on what they already believe about future value. If you can determine on a collective basis what will validate or invalidate those beliefs, then you will know how each group is likely to behave.

I want to remind you that this approach is to help you stay detached and understand that price movement is a function of traders acting individually and collectively as a force expressing their beliefs in future value. The greatest number with the strongest belief will always be right. The easiest way to make money is to go with the flow. To identify the flow, you need to stand apart from the crowd and suspend what you believe about relative value so that you can determine who is likely to do what and with how much force, how is everyone else likely to react, and if it doesn't happen, what will traders do then?

By asking yourself these questions you are automatically keeping your focus of attention on the market and what the possibilities are. Any limitations you place on the market's behavior will cause you to focus on the impossibility instead of the possibility of something happening. Your belief that the market has to behave in certain ways proscribed by your mental structure will cause you to focus your attention on what the market is doing to you, and if what it is doing is causing pain, then the potential exists for you to avoid or distort information, usually resulting in a painful forced awareness.

STEP SIX: LEARNING TO BE OBJECTIVE

To achieve a state of objectivity you need to operate out of beliefs that allow for anything to happen, as opposed to beliefs that allow only for the market to express itself in a limited fashion. If you operate out of a belief that anything can happen, then whatever does happen won't be threatening to you in any way, thereby causing you to avoid or distort certain categories of market information. Any limits you place on the market's behavior will be a compensating factor for your lack of trust and confidence to act appropriately in any given situation. This will be evidenced by the fear, stress, and anxiety that you will feel when the market expresses itself beyond your mental limits and you can't do anything to control the situation.

However, you do have to have some belief or expectation about the future or you wouldn't ever put on a trade in the first place. To be objective, you will need to release yourself from "demand-backed expectations" and make what I call "uncommitted assessments of the probabilities." Unlike the markets, in our everyday social lives we can and do exert control over the environment to assure ourselves of the outcomes that we desire. The rules we learn to abide by in order to interact with one another are our expectations about the future. Once we learn these rules, especially if we have learned them in a painful way, we can demand certain outcomes from the environment. Hence, our expectations of the future are actually demands that the environment conform to our expectations of it. Without really thinking about it, we will carry these same kinds of demands with us into the trading environment because of our natural resistance to letting go of our expectations. That is, staying committed to any limited belief about the possibilities that exist in the markets is virtually the same as making a demand.

If you have any doubts about this, consider that if we weren't demanding that the market conform to our expectations, then we wouldn't ever have a reason to get angry when it doesn't. Have you ever gotten angry at the market? Anger is a natural defense mechanism. When we feel anger, it is an indication that the environment is assaulting us in some way, creating an imbalance between the mental and outer environments. The outer environment is either showing us something about itself or ourselves that we don't want to accept. We protect ourselves with our anger to ward off this assault. In our everyday lives our anger can be an effective tool to get what we want (change what the outer environment is showing us about itself that we can't accept) or to ward off what the environment is showing us about ourselves that we can't accept.

However, if we interact with the market with demand-backed or committed expectations of its behavior, we will cut ourselves off from the information that we need to make accurate assessments of its potential to move in any given direction. If we don't have the power to control the markets in such a way as to make them do what we expect them to do and at the same time we aren't willing to give up our expectations and accept the way things are, then it would create what would otherwise be an irreconcilable dilemma if it weren't for our ability to distort, alter, or exclude information from our awareness. Perceptual distortion is the one compensating factor that will, at least temporarily, correct the imbalance between what we expect and what the market is offering, when there is a difference between the two.

Our committed expectations about the future will act as a force on our perception of market information to control its flow into our mental system in such a way as to avoid a confrontation with anything that doesn't conform with what we already believe is possible.

Which, of course, is always going to be less than what is possible from the market's perspective. If we are perceiving much less than what is available, then we are out of touch with what is possible from the market's perspective and setting ourselves up for a painful forced awareness. To be objective you have to make "uncommitted assessments of the probabilities." Which simply means that you have no commitment to any particular outcome. You just observe what is happening in each moment as an indication of what will probably happen next.

Here is what objectivity feels like, so that you can recognize when you have achieved it.

You feel no pressure to do anything

You have no feeling of fear

You feel no sense of rejection

There is no right or wrong

You recognize that this is what the market is telling me, this is what I do

You can observe the market from the perspective as if you were not in a position, even when you are

You are not focused on money but on the structure of the market

To stay objective anticipate as many possibilities as you can and how probable each of these possibilities are. Then decide in advance what you are going to do in each situation. If none of your scenarios is working out as you anticipated, then get out. Release yourself from the need to be right. The more uncommitted your assessments are the less potential for distortion and experiencing a painful forced awareness.

STEP SEVEN: LEARNING TO MONITOR YOURSELF

As outlined in the exercise to develop self-discipline in Chapter 14, you need to start paying attention to what you are thinking about and what market information you are focused on.

Trading Rules

When you are in a trade constantly ask yourself if anything "has to happen." Obviously, you want the market to go in your direction; however, what I want you to do is monitor how you feel, your level of commitment to what has to happen. Remember there is a big difference in perspective between "what is happening" and something that "has to happen." If you find that your commitment levels are rising, keep on telling youself that it is all right for anything to happen because you are confident in your ability to respond appropriately to whatever does happen.

Ask yourself what can't happen? What can't the market do? When you find yourself rationalizing the market's behavior to support your position, you are operating in the realm of illusion and setting yourself up for a painful forced awareness. Remember the market can do anything, even take your profits away if you allow it. Always take something out of the markets when you find yourself in a winning trade.

A question to ask yourself is if you are prepared to give yourself money today. If the answer doesn't come back a resounding yes, then find out why before you trade. If you can't reconcile the issue or set it aside, then you would be better off not trading, until you do. If you are determined to trade anyway, at the very least make a substantial reduction in the number of contracts you normally trade.

When you find yourself focused on the monetary value of a trade instead of the structure of the market (i.e., what the trade is worth to you in dollar terms, dreams, goals, and so forth instead of what the market is telling you about its potential to move in any given direction) then assume you are distorting or avoiding certain information and either don't put the trade on or take what you have off until you become more objective.

CHAPTER 17

Final Note

Even after you have learned all of the skills set forth in this book, at some point in time it will probably occur to you that your trading is simply a feedback mechanism to tell you how much you like yourself in any given moment. After you have learned to trust yourself to always act in your best interests, the only thing that will hold you back is your degree of self-valuation. That is, you will give yourself an amount of money that directly corresponds with what you believe you deserve based on some value system you acquired at some point in your life. The more positive you feel about yourself, the more abundance that will naturally flow your way as a by-product of these positive feelings. So, in essence, to give yourself more money as a trader you need to identify, change or decharge anything in your mental environment that doesn't contribute to the highest degree of self-valuation that is possible. What's possible? Stay focused on what you need to learn, do the work that is necessary, and your belief in what is possible will naturally expand as a function of your willingness to adapt.

Index

A

Accountability, 50
Accumulation of profits, 72
Active loser concept, 43-44
  loss cutting and, 65-66
Adaptation:
  acknowledgement of need to learn,
    130-31
  constant state of learning, 148
  current knowledge as block to new
    knowledge, 130-36
  to environmental conditions,
    121-37
  learning and quality of experiences,
    126-37
  and level of satisfaction, 121-22
  of mental environment to known
    physical world, 125-26
  mental techniques, 148
  obsolescence of old knowledge,
    136-37
Affirmations and trading, 177
Anger:
  defusion of, 156
  and demand for market
    conformation, 220
  in mental environment, 87
Associations, 103-09
  categorization, 103
  energy loop and, 105-09
  extraneous sensory information,
    103-04
  individuality of, 108
  natural, 133-34
  positive and negative experiences,
    104
Attention:
  directed, by writing, 172-73
  energy intensity and, 115
  limiting to single market behavior,
    208-10
Attractions, and learning, 126-27

B

Balance area, 190-93
  versus "value area," 190-91
Bear market requirements, price
  dynamics, 199-200

Behavior, cultural, *see* Cultural
  behavior; Market behavior
Being wrong, 46
  change of beliefs, 12
  and market sense, 47
  and personal belief system, 46
Belief alteration techniques, 167-79
  affirmations, 177-79
  desire for change, 167-68
  indentification of conflicting
    beliefs, 169-71
  self-discipline development, 173-77
  self-hypnosis, 177
  writing for attention direction,
    172-73
Beliefs, 113-15
  about deserving money, 17
  change about being wrong, 12
  child's definition of reality, 131-32
  as closed-loop system, 113-14
  comfort zone and, 168
  in conflict with goals, 173
  cultural, detriment to trading,
    15-16
  de-energized, 168
  distortion of, 22-23
  as emotional energy, 87
  as environmental information
    management systems,
    113-15
  erroneous, locked into, 18
  and fire walkers, 16
  formed from experiences, 131-32
  indestructibility of, 168
  and information inhibition,
    114-15
  limiting, 28-29, 68-69
  limiting ability to gather
    information, 39-40
  manipulation techniques, 82
  parameter definition, 114
  in probable outcome, 214
  resistance implied in, 25-27
  as self-fulfilling prophecies, 194
  significance of losses, 12
  "trading is easy," 22-23
  versus conscious goals, 173
  versus intents, 145
  see also Personal belief systems
Bid, defined, 184

Bull market requirements, 199-200
Buyer and seller ratio, 39
Buying force, creation of, 191-92

C

Change, mental environment and,
  136-37
Charged energy:
  fear and, 102-03
  intensity of, 100-03
  memories, 100-03
  polarity of, 100
  "quality of energy," 100
  see also Negatively charged energy;
    Positively charged energy
Childhood conditioning, and money,
  17
Collective behavior of traders, 51-52
  price dynamics, 187
  price movement and, 60-61
Comfort zone of beliefs, 168
Competition and price movement, 60
Competitive environment, 17
Confidence:
  increased sense of, 161-62
  wisdom and, 164
Conflicting beliefs, identification of,
  169-71
Confusion, in mental environment, 87
Conscious goals *versus* beliefs, 173
Creation of market experience,
  66-69, 202
Creativity, 157-59
  destructive life cycles and, 157-58
  in mental environment, 87
  mental growth and, 157
  self-limiting rules and, 158
  self-recreation and, 159
Crowd anticipation, and trading
  choices, 54
Cultural behavior:
  errors of, *versus* trading skills, 18-20
  and trading environment, 16-18
  see also Cultural thought
    methodology
Cultural thought methodology:
  childhood conditioning, 17

cultural environment *versus* trading environment, 18
distortion of beliefs, 22–23
effort concept, 17, 22
expertise concept, 22
fear of financial ruin, 17
feelings of failure, 23
focus on price, 19
money concepts, 17
need to win, 17
psychological impact of market environment, 17
reward concept, 17, 22
self-confrontation, 17
structured work beliefs, 17–18
time concept, 17, 22
trading errors *versus* trading skills, 18–20
"trading is easy" belief, 22–23
versus thought methodology of trading, 15–30
see also Trading methodology
Current knowledge, as block to new knowledge, 130–36
Current price:
defined, 35
market perception and, 66–67
Current set of limitations, 130–36
and learning, 136–37
Cycles:
environmental, 95
of fear, 102–03
of market reversal, 194–95
and price movement, 192

D

"Demand-backed expectations," 219
Developing trading skills, 201–22
banishment of fear, 202
capital as tuition, 206
change of focus, 204
concentration on single market behavior, 208–10
executing losing trades, 207–08
execution of trading system, 210–13
focus on learning, 204–06
identification of guidelines, 203

learning objectivity, 219–21
losses, dealing with, 206–08
need for self-trust, 203
outguessing system, 211–13
predefining losses, 206–07
redefining missed opportunities, 205
redefining "mistakes," 204–05
self-examination, 216
self-monitoring, 221
skill identification, 202
thinking in probabilities, 215–19
trading experience framework, 205
trading system problems, 211
see also Trading skills
Disciplined trader, *see* Successful trader
Disciplined trading approach, 70
Discomfort from inconsistent actions, 173
Disequilibrium, creation of, 191–92
Distinctions:
environmental, 104, 108
perceptual, 105–07
Distortion:
of beliefs, 22–23
of information, freedom from, 203
of perception, 22
Dreams:
and market's power over, 17
in mental environment, 87, 91–94
nondimensionality of, 91–92
speed of, 92–94

E

Economic law of supply and demand, 61–62
and price movement, 62
Effort concept, 17, 22
Emotional control, needed for trading skills, 4
Emotional energy, *see* Mental energy
Emotional wounds, 142–43
Emotions, 87
anger, 156, 220
categories of, 87
fear, *see* Fear

Emotions (*Continued*)
  greed, 46
  positively and negatively charged,
      87, 101–03
  relationship with perceptions,
      110–13
  revenge, 46–47
  stress, *see* Stress
Energy loop:
  associations and, 105–09
  perceptual distinctions, 105–07
Environmental cycles, 95
Environmental distinctions, 104
  individuality of, 108
Environmental information:
  perceptual distinctions, 105–08
  processed as experience, 89–91
Environmental information
      management systems, 99–119
  associations, 103–09
  beliefs, 113–15
  energy loop between physical and
      mental environments,
      105–09
  fear as negative situation enhancer,
      115–19
  memory storage, 99–103
  relationship between perceptions
      and emotions, 110–13
Environments:
  cultural *versus* trading, 16–18
  mental, *see* Mental environment
  unstructured, of market, 49–57
Equilibrium of market, 184
Equity charting, as state of mind,
      153–54
Exchange system, money as, 61
Execution of trades, as trading skill,
      71–72
Expectations:
  "demand-backed," 219
  in mental environment, 87
  public *versus* professional, 200
Experience:
  defined, 89
  environmental information
      processed as, 89–91
  internal impetus for shaping of, 109
  quality of, and learning, 126–37
Expertise concept, 22

F

Failure, feelings of, 23
Fear, 115–19
  affecting market judgement, 117–19
  as attention limiter, 115
  charged energy and, 102–03
  choice limitations in trading,
      118–19
  creating more fear, 116–17
  and cultural thought methodology,
      16–17
  cycles of, 102–03
  evolution beyond, 202
  of financial devastation, 17
  and force of pain recognition, 108
  immobilization by, 19
  limiting force, 102–03
  losing trade and, 118
  from opposition of intents and
      beliefs, 145
  and perception of choice, 82–83
  price movement and, 82
  purpose of, 116
  release of, 70–71
  supply and demand and, 61–62
  winning trade and, 118
Fear generation:
  and ability to execute trade, 71–72
  author's, 9
  from psychological damage, 71
Feelings:
  categories of, in mental
      environment, 87
  and time perception, 97–98
Fire walkers, 16
Framework for trading experiences,
      205
Future value:
  defined, 63
  as trading rationale, 63–64

G

Gambling:
  and active loser concept, 43–44
  versus trading, 43, 212

Goal achievement dynamics, 139–54
  constant state of learning, 149
  fundamental assumptions, 149–50
  with insufficient skills, 141
  interaction skill level, 140–41
  need for learning, 19
  need recognition and, 139
  perfection of moment, 150–53
  recognition of need to learn,
    149–50
  rewards at self-valuation levels,
    153–54
Goals:
  changing opportunities for
    fulfillment, 162
  in conflict with beliefs, 173
  conscious, *versus* beliefs, 173
  formulation of, 139
  interaction with external
    environment, 139
  in mental environment, 87
  see also Goal achievement
    dynamics
Greed:
  defined, 46
  in mental environment, 87
  origin of, 41–42
  and personal belief system, 46
  supply and demand and, 61–62
Guilt, feelings of, 23

H

Hedging:
  effect on market, 192
  and value protection, 192
Herd mentality of traders, 51–52
Hesitation, and opportunity
    perception, 218
Highs:
  market testing, 195
  price movement, 193
Holograms, as example of
    nondimensionality of energy,
    91
Hoping:
  value of, 164
  versus intuition, 163

I

Identity, valid symbols of, 9
Illusions, 151–52
  defined, 151
  in mental environment, 87
Inadequacy, feelings of, 23
Inconsistent actions, discomfort and
    resistance from, 173
Individual traders:
  experiences and market perception,
    66–67
  and price dynamics, 187
Insults, escalation of, 155
Intensity of energy, 100–03
Intent *versus* beliefs, 143–44
  in trading, 144–45
Interdependency of trade system,
    61–62
Intuition:
  ignoring of, 19
  in mental environment, 87
  increase of, 163–64
  versus wishing or hoping, 163

K

Knowledge:
  evolution, 159–60
  impossibility of perfection, 128
  non-existence of mistakes, 160

L

Last posted price, defined, 184
Learning:
  assessment of probabilities, 132–33
  experience quality and, 126–37
  as function of human existence,
    127–28
  necessity for constant state, 147–48
  need to know, 126
  need to learn, 126–27
  see also Adaptation
  versus resistance, 162–63

Limiting beliefs, 28–29, 68–69
Losing:
  and cultural assumptions, 39–40
  and market sense, 47
  passive loser *versus* active loser
    concepts, 43–44
  personal belief system, 46
  random, 54
Losing trade:
  execution of, 207–08
  and market temptation, 42
  refusal to liquidate, 18
Loss cutting, active loser concept,
  65–66
Losses:
  acceptance of, 25
  consequences of avoidance, 11
  from culturally learned behavior,
    18–19
  dealing with, 206–08
  predefining, 206–07
  refusing definition of, 18
Lows:
  market testing, 195
  price movement, 193

M

Market:
  defined, 35
  efficiency of, 64
  as gamble, 39–40
  offering of opportunity, 202
  perpetual motion of, 217
  psychological perspective, 27
  randomness of, 64
  rightness of, 35–37
  temptations of, 42
  testing of, 195
  as unstructured environment,
    49–57
Market behavior, 27, 188–89
  and beliefs, 36–37
  concentration on single, 208–10
  defined, 188
  patterns, 188–89
  price patterns and formations,
    190–93
Market data organization, 190

Market environment, 17
  psychological impact of, 17
  "unlimitedness," 39–40
  unstructured, 49–57
Market experience, creation of,
  66–69
Market interaction and traders, 37
Market movement, perception of
  opportunity and, 68–69
  see also Price movement
Market movement assessment:
  limit on information gathered, by
    erroneous, 39–40
  psychological factors, 40
Market participant consistency,
  defined, 39
Market perception, individual
  experiences and, 66–67
Market position, *see* Positions of
  traders
Market potential, focus on, 19
Market temptations on winning and
  losing trades, 42
Market value, determination of, 35
Memories:
  as behavioral force, 98
  as charged energy, 100–03
  compression of, 97
  as environmental information
    systems, 100–03
  fear generating, 102–03
  in mental environment, 91–94
  nondimensionality of, 91–92
  painful, 102–03
  significant, 96–97
  speed of, 92–94
  versus recollection, 141–42
Mental energy:
  defined, 88–89
  expression of, 87
  management of, *see* Mental energy
    management
  negatively charged, 101–03, 155
  positively charged, 101
Mental energy management, 155–65
  anger diffusion, 156
  benefits, 161–65
  constructive thoughts, 156
  destructive thoughts, 155
  increased levels of satisfaction,
    162–63

increased sense of security, 161–62
insults, 155
negatively charged energy, 155
and escalation of emotions, 155–56
tools for change, 156–57
Mental environment, 85–98
balance with outer physical
environment, 122
brain and, 90
categories in, 87
changes for effective functioning,
136–37
correspondence to energy, 91–98
definition, 87–88
dreams, 92
framework of mental environment,
87
memories, 91–94
nature of, 85–87
nondimensionality, 91–92
speed of, 92–98
thoughts, 156–57
time and, 94–96
Mental growth at conscious level,
157
"Mistakes":
non-existence of, 160–61
redefinition of, 204–05
Moment perfection, 150–53
Money:
childhood conditioning about
"deserving," 17
defined, 61
how traders make, 184
as system of exchange, 61
windfall profits *versus* structured
work beliefs, 17–18

N

Natural association, 133–34
see also Associations
Needs:
in mental environment, 87
recognition of, 139
Need to learn:
determination of, 129–30
difficulty of acknowledgement
of, 130

Negatively charged energy:
anger, 156
categories of, 87
characteristics, 101–03
fear, *see* Fear
greed, *see* Greed
revenge, 46–47
stress, *see* Stress
Non-physical *versus* physical reality,
90

O

Objectivity, 219–22
developing trading skills, 219–21
recognition of, 221
and trading rules, 222
and "uncommitted assessments of
probabilities", 219–21
Offer, defined, 184
Opportunity:
identification of, 202
and inability to execute trade, 218
missed, redefining, 205
Opportunity perception, 69–71
execution failure and, 72
and market movement, 68–69
as trading skill, 69–71

P

Passive loser concept, 43–47
Passive losers, and price movement,
44–47
Perceptions:
alternate experiences and, 111–13
blocking by current belief, 133
changing, and trading, 135–36
experience shaping and, 107–09
of opportunity, *see* Opportunity
perception
relationship with emotion,
110–13
total environmental distinctions
and, 107
of traders, and price movement,
64

Perceptual distinctions:
  and energy loops, 105–07
  environmental information,
    105–07
  market opportunities, 106
Perceptual diversity of individuals,
  135
Perpetual motion:
  of market, 217
  of market, and passive loser
    concept, 43–47
  of prices, 41–47
Personal belief systems, 46–47
  being wrong, 46
  choice range, 171
  conflicting belief identification,
    169–71
  directing conscious shift, 167–69
  greed, 46
  losing, 46
  revenge, 46–47
  techniques for change, see Belief
    alteration techniques
Physical versus non-physical reality,
  90
Point and figure charts, 187
Polarity of energy, 100–03
Positions of traders:
  and determination to keep, 19
  price movement and, 59
Positively charged energy:
  characteristics, 101
  in mental environment, 87
Present value agreement, 184
Price charts, 187
  significant market reference points,
    189–90
  symmetrical patterns, 189
Price dynamics, 184–88
  bear market requirements,
    199–200
  bull market requirements,
    199–200
  collective behavior of traders, 187
  highs and lows, 193
  individual traders and, 187
  market behavior, 188–89
  price patterns and formations,
    190–93
  public versus professional
    expectations, 200

reversal of support and resistance
  levels, 196–97
shift of balance of force, 187, 194
significant market reference points,
  189–90
support and resistance, 193–97
trends and trendlines, 197–200
Price movement:
  collective behavior of traders and,
    60–61
  competition and, 60
  direction, 218
  effect of personal belief, 36
  function of group behavior, 187
  highs and lows, 193
  market behavior patterns, 188–89
  meanings of, 27
  opportunity creation, 36
  passive losers and, 44–47
  perpetual, 41
  price patterns and formations,
    190–93
  probability and, 44–45
  profit opportunity from, 11
  psychology of, 183–200
  risks and, 62
  supply and demand and, 62
  support and resistance value levels,
    193–97
  traders' perceptions and, 64
  traders' positions and, 59
  trading rules and, 8, 206–08
Price patterns and formations,
  190–93
  balance area, 190–93
  "value area" versus balance area,
    190–91
Probabilities:
  and price movement, 44–45
  thinking in, 215–19
Probability assessment:
  of learning, 132–33
  uncommitted, 69–70
Profit accumulation, 72
Profit and loss potential, 39–40
Psychological damage, defined, 71
Psychological factors:
  market movement assessment, 40
  of trading success, 27–30
Psychological impact of market
  interaction on individual, 17

Q

"Quality of energy," 100

R

Random winning and losing, 54
Rationale of author, 3–13
Reasoning ability, mental growth and, 157
Reasons:
  irrelevance of, in market environment, 59–64
  for trading, 61–62
Recollection *versus* memories, 141–42
Reference points, *see* Significant market reference points
Release of fear, 70–71
Resistance:
  formed from inconsistent actions, 173
  versus learning, 162–63
Resistance price level, 193–97
  becoming support price level, 196–97
  defined, 193
  identified, 195
Responsibility:
  avoidance of, through lack of structure, 52–53
  avoidance of, through superstition, 53–54
  and self-acceptance, 55
  taking of, 46
  taking of, in unstructured environment, 49–57
Revenge:
  and market sense, 47
  and personal belief system, 46–47
Reward concept, 17, 22
Rightness of market, 35–37
Risks:
  defined, 62
  gambling *versus* trading, 212
  and price movement, 62
Rule establishment in unstructured environment, 49–50
Rules for trading, *see* Trading rules

S

Satisfaction, increased levels of, 162–63
Security, increased sense of, 161–62
Self-acceptance, 55, 72–77
  example of failure, 73–76
  responsibility and, 55
  results of cultivation, 77
Self-discipline:
  belief alteration techniques, 173–77
  defined, 201
  exercises, 174–77
  lack of, 29–30
  need of, for trading skills, 4
  and trading, 201
Self-hypnosis and new belief establishment, 177
Self-improvement, need of traders, 151–53
Self-knowledge, 10
Self-monitoring, and developing trading skills, 221–22
Self-trust, in developing trading skills, 203
Self-valuation:
  profit accumulation and, 72
  and trading, 223
  as trading skill, 72
Set of limitations, current, 128–29
Shame, feelings of, 23
Significant market reference points, 189–90
  defined, 189
  determination of, 216–17
  establishment, 194
  highs and lows, 193
  price charts, 189
  support and resistance, 193–97
Social thought methodology, *see* Cultural thought methodology
Static environment and sense of well-being, 17
Stress:
  defined, 131
  as learning device, 135
  in mental environment, 87
  in trading environment, 17

Structured work beliefs *versus*
    windfall profits, 17–18
Successful trader, 65–77
    change of mental perspective, 162
    creation of market experience,
        66–69
    disciplined trading approach, 70
    evolution beyond fear, 202
    internal changes, necessity of, 5–6
    perception of opportunities, 69–71
    profit accumulation, 72
    release of fear, 70–71
    self-acceptance, 72–77
    technique explanation, difficulty
        of, 4–6
    trade execution, 71–72
    winning trade, and fear, 202
Superstition as trading factor, 53–54
Supply and demand, 61–62
Support and resistance zone, defined,
    195
Support price level, 193–97
    becoming resistance price level,
        196–97
    defined, 193
    identified, 195

T

Thinking ability:
    as greatest asset, 10
    mental growth and, 157
Thought methodology of trading, *see*
    Trading methodology
Thought methodology, social and
    cultural, 15–30
Thoughts:
    constructive, 156
    destructive, 155
    in mental environment, 87
    as tools for change, 156–57
Time:
    concept, 17, 22
    defined, 95
    experiences of, and feelings, 97–98
    individuality of perception of,
        108–09
    mental environment and, 95

and reward principles, 17
and space, 95
subjective measurement of, 95–96
Traders:
    cultural beliefs *versus* trading
        success, 18–19
    disciplined, *see* Successful trader
    equity charting as state of mind,
        153–54
    and interaction with market, 37
    irrelevance of reasons, 59–64
    as market components, 184
    relating to value, 191
    self-improvement needs, 151–53
    self-valuation, 154
    successful, *see* Successful trader
    unsuccessful, *see* Unsuccessful
        trader
Trades:
    as indicators of self-evaluation,
        153–54
    execution of, 71–72
    and market consistency, 36
    and potential for market
        movement, 36
Trading:
    creating of market experience, 202
    decision possibilities, 41–42
    defined, 63
    goal of, 63–64
    interdependency of, 61–62
    learning flawless execution of,
        213–14
    as mental activity, 201–02
    psychological factors of success,
        27–30
    reasons for, 61–62
    and self-discipline, 201
    and self-valuation, 223
    structural lack and responsibility
        avoidance, 52–53
    trial and error approach to, 4–5
    see also Trading environment;
        Trading skills
Trading environment:
    collective behavior, 51–52, 60–61
    immediacy of outcome and, 67–68
    psychological issues for individual
        trader, 42
    nature of, 35–77

perpetual motion of prices, 41–47
profit and loss potential, 39–40
rightness of market, 35–37
and stress, 17
unlimitedness of, 39–40
unstructured environment, 49–57
versus cultural environment, 16–18
Trading methodology, 15–30
effort concept, 17, 22
reasons for adopting, 25–27
release of feelings of failure, 23
reward concept, 17, 22
skill acquisition, 19–20
and system validity, 21
time concept, 17, 22
and trading errors, 18–19
and trading systems, 20–21
in unlimited environment, 23
see also Cultural thought
methodology
Trading pattern, result of consistency
of, 19
Trading range:
defined, 195
and money-making technique,
195–96
Trading rules, 12, 206–08
establishment in unstructured
environment, 49–50
exact implementation, 214
following, as trading skill, 203–04
money management, 12
Trading skills, 19–20, 69–72
accumulation of profits, 72
belief alteration and, 23–27
creation of market experience,
66–69, 202
emotional control, 4
establishing trading rules, 203
execution of trades, 71–72
flawless execution of trading
system, 210–13
focus on "now moment," 216
following trading rules, 203–04
freedom from information
distortion, 203
identification of, 202
lack of, 28
perception of opportunity, 69–71,
202

psychological beliefs and, 21–23
self-discipline, 4, 201
self-trust, 203
self-valuation, 72
thinking in probabilities, 215–19
trading without fear, 202
versus cultural behavior, 18–19
versus trading systems, 20–21
see also Developing trading skills
Trading systems:
adherence to, 214
defined, 211
establishment of, 213–14
ignoring rules of, 19
and loss tolerance, 213
and market behavior, 20
objectives, 213–14
outguessing, 211–13
problems with, 211
versus trading methodology,
20–21
Training exercise:
belief in probable outcome, 214
objectives of, 213
Trends:
defined, 197
as function of time, 197–98
Trial and error approach to trading,
4–5
Trust and wisdom, 164

U

"Uncommitted assessments of
probabilities," 219–20
necessary for effective trading,
69–70
Understanding and wisdom, 164
Unstructured environment, 49–57
rule establishment in, 49–50
taking of responsibility in, 49–57
Unsuccessful traders:
and belief alteration, 23–27
childhood conditioning about
deserving money, 17
and culturally-learned behavior,
18–19
forced awareness of failure, 6–7

Unsuccessful traders (*Continued*)
  impact of cultural environment,
     16–18
  inability to adapt, 162
  lack of self-discipline, 29–30
  lack of skills, 28
  limiting beliefs, 25–26, 28–29
  mental inflexibility, 162
  winning trade, and fear, 202
  see also Successful trader
Unsuccessful trading, 28–30

V

Validation symbols, and trader's
  "identity," 9
"Value area" *versus* balance area,
  190–91
Value, monetary, focus on, 19

W

Windfall profits *versus* structured
  work beliefs, 17–18
Winning, random, 54
Winning trade:
  and fear, 202
  and market temptation, 42
Wisdom:
  as benefit of mental energy
     management, 164–65
  change of polarity and, 164–65
Wishing:
  value of, 164
  versus intuition, 163
Writing, to direct attention, for belief
  alteration, 172–73